# BACKYARD MAINE

# BACKYARD MAINE

Local Essays by Edgar Allen Beem

TILBURY HOUSE PUBLISHERS
Gardiner, Maine

Tilbury House, Publishers
103 Brunswick Avenue
Gardiner, Maine 04345
800–582–1899 • www.tilburyhouse.com

First paperback edition: March 2009
10 9 8 7 6 5 4 3 2 1

Most of these pieces have appeared in *The Forecaster* in Edgar Allen
Beem's "The Universal Notebook" column. Others, as noted, were previ-
ously published in *Maine Times*.

Library of Congress Cataloging-in-Publication Data
Beem, Edgar Allen, 1949-
  Backyard Maine : local essays / by Edgar Allen Beem. -- 1st pbk. ed.
     p. cm.
  ISBN 978-0-88448-317-5 (pbk. : alk. paper)
  1. Maine--Anecdotes. 2. Beem, Edgar Allen, 1949---Anecdotes. I.
Title.
  F26.B44 2009
  974.1'043--dc22
                              2008045205

Cover photograph by Tess Beem
Cover design by Geraldine Millham, Westport, Massachusetts
Copyediting by Genie Dailey, Fine Points Editorial Services, Jefferson,
     Maine
Printed and bound by Versa Press, East Peoria, Illinois

Dedicated to the memories of
Peter W. Cox and John N. Cole,
co-founders of *Maine Times*.
Peter gave me my start as a journalist
and John gave me his column in *The Forecaster*,
from whence came these essays.

# CONTENTS

# INTRODUCTION

The majority of the essays collected here first appeared in "The Universal Notebook," my column in *The Forecaster,* a free-circulation weekly newspaper serving Greater Portland, Maine. The title of my column is taken from the Universal Note Book, a 4 x 8-inch spiral-bound reporter's notebook that fits in just about any pocket and sells for $18.95 a dozen. I order them two dozen at a time from a stationer in Richmond, Virginia, there's a stack of thirty-five used ones on my desk representing a year's worth of work, there's another hundred or so old notebooks piled on the bookcase across the room, and there are hundreds more tucked away in boxes down in the basement, the by-products of a life spent scribbling for a living.

The Universal Note Books in the basement only date back to 1981 when I went to work for the now defunct alternative weekly *Maine Times* as an art critic and feature writer. A handful of the longer essays in this collection were culled from *Maine Times.* I actually started my journalism career (if that's what it turns out to be) back in 1965 when, after my sophomore year at Westbrook High School, I became the school reporter for the old *Westbrook American*. The first feature article I turned in—an account of my English teacher Altie Hayden's summer vacation in Europe—was written in longhand on lined theme paper. Bob Morehead, a cocky young editor right out of the University of Alabama and destined to edit the *Kennebec Journal*, kicked it right back to me.

"Type it up!"

I had never used a typewriter before, so I randomly hunted and pecked my way through my first published article, much the same way I do forty-four years and a few thousand bylines later. Of course, now I hunt and peck with professional velocity.

Using a heavy old Smith-Corona manual, I happily clattered and clacked my way through football, basketball, and baseball reports for the *Westbrook American,* book reviews for the *Maine Sunday Telegram,* a weekly column ("On the Other Hand") in the old *Portland Evening Express,* art reviews and a satirical column ("Moto & Guzzi") in the long-dead *Portland Independent,* and art reviews, essays, and feature articles in *Maine Times* until one day in 1986 when, very much against my will, I was forced to start writing on a word processor.

I was reluctant to enter the digital age not only because I am deeply skeptical of technology but also because I had discovered that two decades of typing had left me barely able to write legibly by hand. These days, even I can't read my handwriting.

Writing on a manual typewriter had forced a certain discipline on my thinking. I'd carefully outline every piece of writing beforehand (using a method taught to me by my eighth-grade English teacher Miss Frances Weeks) so that when I began typing, I had all the facts, quotes, and transitions in place. Typing was just a matter of wordsmithing. I quickly discovered that a word processor allows you to just dump everything in—notes, quotes, ideas—then move things around until they make sense. It's a heck of a lot easier, but it still feels chaotic and somehow dishonest to me.

Since I left *Maine Times* in 1995, I have been keyboarding and mousing my way through articles for *Down East, Yankee, Boston Globe Magazine, ARTnews, Photo District News,* and just about anyone else who'll pay me. It still makes me uneasy, however, that when I hit SEND my carefully chosen words disappear into the ether, only to reappear weeks and months later in print. I'm not sure I completely understand how this happens.

Given the delay between submission and publication, I am always running into folks at Hannafords or Shaw's supermarkets who'll say, "Hey, I saw your article in—*fill-in-the-blank.*" I often have no idea what they've read, because I wrote the piece so long ago and have written six or eight more stories in the meantime. That's one of the main reasons I was so pleased to be asked to write a weekly column for *The Forecaster.* I sit here in my Yarmouth sunroom/office each weekend hunting and pecking out 600–700 words that I then e-mail down to Falmouth on Monday. Come Thursday, my friends and neighbors know exactly what's on my mind at the moment, and I know exactly what they've read. There's a lot to be said for being local.

# SPRING

## IN PRAISE OF WOMAN

On March 25, my lovely wife Carolyn turns—well, suffice it to say next Tuesday is her birthday. Since the only serious fault she has is the fact that she is nearly impossible to buy a present for, I thought this year I'd give her something she can't return or exchange—a public declaration of my undying love.

When I first set eyes on Carolyn, she was a seventeen-year-old student at Portland High School, a cute kid in a mischievous sort of way. I, eight years her senior, was a librarian at Portland Public Library. No one, including myself, could have predicted that six years later the lecherous old librarian would be married to that beautiful brown-eyed girl. Twenty-nine years and three daughters later, I am truly amazed on a daily basis at the woman she has become.

I admit it, I fell in love with Carolyn primarily because she was cute and sexy. I quickly discovered that she was also bright, funny, irreverent, didn't take herself too seriously, and generally shared my view of the world—or I wouldn't have quit my job at the library in 1980 to follow her to Winchester, England, where she was finishing college and where we were married in a whirlwind ceremony that required us to invite a total stranger to be one of our witnesses.

Today, everything I have in the world I have because of her. We have this little house in Yarmouth because Carolyn took the initiative to sign up for a Farmer's Home Administration loan when I was making beans as a freelancer (I now make three beans) while trying to write a novel. We have three wonderful daughters because, despite my initial fear of fatherhood, Carolyn was ready to have babies. And I have the luxury of staying home and pecking out a living on this computer, because Carolyn has a good job at L.L. Bean with all the necessary benefits.

I confess that when we were first married I figured that, being older, possessed of a graduate degree, a journalist wise in the ways of the world, I would mold this little filly into a woman who shared my tastes in art and literature and politics. Think again, foolish man! I was still laboring under the old paradigm where the man was the chief breadwinner, king of his castle, etc., and the woman was the homemaker and stay-at-home mom. Well, a few years after we were married, Carolyn took a part-time job at L.L. Bean for the Christmas season, just to bring in a little extra money. That part-time job turned into a full-time job, then a supervisory position, then the primary means of support for our growing family.

Along the way, L.L. Bean sent Carolyn to the Muskie Institute to earn a master's degree in public policy, so that she now spends her days monitoring environmental, labor, tax, and postal issues for Bean and dealing with the crack-pots who target L.L. Bean whenever something happens in Maine they don't like. I have to believe that the reason she is so patient and reasonable when fielding irate calls that come out of left field has something to do with the fact that she is married to a crackpot.

Sometimes, in fact, I have to wonder what Carolyn sees in me. I stay at home and write and complain. I go to various meetings, watch sports, and cart our youngest daughter around. That's about it. Oh, I do most of the grocery shopping and cook most of the meals, but she does all the baking, pays all the bills, prepares the taxes, tends the garden, paints and wallpapers, runs three to five miles a day, works out at the Y, and still finds time to read more than I do. She loves to travel. I love to stay home. When she's sick (which is rare), you wouldn't know it, and when I'm sick everyone knows it. I swear she gave birth to three children without uttering a sound.

So, guys, allow me to clue you in here—not only is the love of your life probably more interesting than you give her credit for, she's probably more interesting than you are. Yes, I'm a sexist. I believe women are infinitely stronger, smarter, and wiser than men. We'd be a hell of a lot better off these days if there were a woman in the White House. And Carolyn Barbara Thompson Beem is the reason I think so.

I love you, honey. Happy birthday. I hope that's enough.

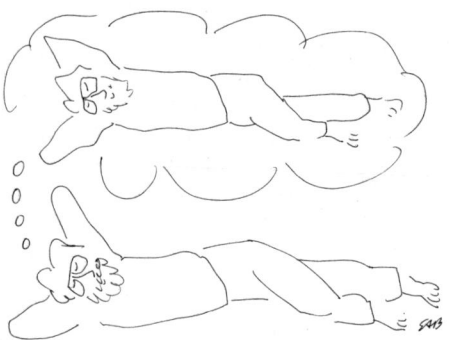

# GETTING ALONG, GETTING AHEAD

Ambition is such an unattractive quality in a person. Certainly there's nothing wrong with wanting to excel, to do the best you can. If you want to become a doctor or a lawyer in order relieve suffering and serve the cause of justice, that's commendable. If you want to become a doctor or a lawyer so you can make big bucks and become financially secure, that's quite another thing; the word contemptible comes first to mind.

There is something deeply troubling about personal ambition, seeking after wealth, fame, and power for their own sakes. It suggests a person is not only self-centered but also lacking a broader vision of human existence. You miss the mystery and the magic if you're focused on the brass ring.

A few years ago, we heard a lot about raising the aspirations of Maine kids, getting them out of the get-along mentality that characterizes those of us who grew up in the old Maine and into the get-ahead mindset of the new Maine.

Low aspirations may still be a problem in the dim mill towns and dying farm communities, but it hasn't been an issue here in the Type A suburbs for decades now. In fact, just the opposite may be the case.

Kids from towns like Cape Elizabeth, Cumberland, Falmouth, and Yarmouth are so driven to succeed that they tend to regard attending a University of Maine System college as something just short of failure. They think of the state university as a bottom-feeder school. They'd rather attend the University of New Hampshire or the University of Vermont than the University of Maine, let alone the University of Southern Maine (my own great and good alma mater).

Truth be told, you can get just as good an education at UMO, USM, or UM-Farmington as you can at Bowdoin, Bates, or Colby. What you're paying for at most expensive private schools are the country-club amenities and the connections. You're buying a pedigree and a network. Of course I say that as a father who has two daughters who will graduate from expensive private schools this spring.

Hannah received her BFA in furniture design from Rhode Island School of Design. She might as well have grown up in the 1960s, because she would have made an excellent hippie. She's never been concerned about getting ahead; she just wants to do her own thing. Nora earned a BS in biology with a concentration in environmental science from Smith. She just finished graduate work at UNH and is turning herself inside out at the moment trying to decide the next move—travel, work, more graduate school, career?

I'm afraid I'm not much help in the career-planning department, because I never planned on having a career.

When I graduated from USM in 1971, I just knew I wanted to write and imagined somehow I would wind up as a novelist. Those stillborn novels are still in boxes in the basement somewhere. When I was Nora's age, I was perfectly happy cleaning offices in Portland, making Italian sandwiches at Eight Corners Market in Scarborough, and then landing a job at Portland Public Library through no real effort of my own. I was actually surprised when I wound up as a journalist (primarily because I was asked, not because I wanted to). I guess I shouldn't have been, because that's exactly what the Kudor Preference Test told me I should be way back in the seventh grade at Westbrook Junior High.

It is quite possible that my distaste for the ambitions of others (I'm also not interested in their dreams, genealogies, or medical conditions) is just a way of rationalizing my own lack of ambition. I never really understood why a reporter is supposed to want to become an editor. I never did. And I always dismissed the advice that I should go to New York City if I wanted to make it as a writer. I figured I already lived where half the people in Manhattan wish they could live. And it was always more important to me to be home when the kids got out of school than to win a Pulitzer Prize. If anyone had ever told me what a racket college teaching is, however, I might have gone on to get a Ph.D. in philosophy. Get a Ph.D., Nora. Teach college. It's a cushy racket.

All that said, however, I should confess that I do have a couple of movie and TV projects in the works. If one of them comes through and I make a ton of money, I'm planning to instantly forget where I come from. To hell with this Podunk town! I'll be out in Hollywood schmoozing with the glitterati. And don't ask me to introduce you to my new friends Jack and Brad and Julia and Johnny. See what I mean about ambition?

# THE MAINE IDEA

As we sit here in the relative safety and sanity of the Pine Tree State and watch in horror and disbelief from afar as the rest of the world careens from crisis into chaos, I can't help thinking that we'd all be better off if the other 6.7 billion folks on Earth got the Maine Idea.

The Maine Idea is just that common sense, moderation, tolerance, and decency should rule the land. There should be a balance between culture and nature, between the personal and the public, between the corporate and the common good. It's ultimately more important to get along in this world than it is to get ahead.

Spare me the pinko liberal socialist letters to the editor. When it comes to common sense, moderation, tolerance, and decency, I claim no superiority for the far left where I happen to hang out. I'm all in favor of the good antiwar work that Camden native and MoveOn.org organizer Eli Pariser does, but I'm also impressed by the good governance crusade of Robert A. G. Monks, who is leading the charge to force

Exxon Mobil to strip its CEO of chairman of the board status. You might expect shareholder advocacy from an Eli Pariser, but Bob Monks is a wealthy Cape Elizabeth Republican.

There aren't many progressive Republicans (Rockefeller Republicans we used to call them) left in this world, but Maine seems to breed more than its fair share. Margaret Chase Smith and her principled stand against McCarthyism. Bill Cohen and his role in the Watergate impeachment hearings. And though I risk having my liberal credentials revoked for saying so, Olympia Snowe and Susan Collins still strike me as moderates as the GOP goes these days.

But I'm not just talking about the Maine political idea. It's the whole normal, neighborly, just-folks nature of Maine. In this celebrity-sick culture, for example, we get our share of self-important narcissists hiding out along the coast, but most who enjoy fame in Maine wear their celebrity very lightly. I think of my old friend, the late, great actor Gary Merrill strolling Scarborough Beach, actress Glenn Close standing in line for Italian sandwiches at Amato's, marathoner Joan Benoit Samuelson coaching Freeport cross-country skiers, novelist Stephen King watching ballgames in Bangor.

The writings of Scott and Helen Nearing and E. B. White helped spread the word about the good life to be had in Maine, attracting both back-to-the-landers and gentlemen farmers in droves. Maine became synonymous with simplicity, honesty, independence. And Maine as a brand came to stand for quality goods handmade by hard-working people. Think L.L. Bean, Bath Iron Works, Hodgdon Yachts, Angela Adams Rugs.

One of Maine's most important exports, however, is

statesmanship, peace-making if you will. When the Iron Curtain finally fell, a lot of people mistakenly gave Ronald Reagan credit for it, but we in Maine knew that it was a little Maine schoolgirl named Samantha Smith who laid the groundwork for peace with her common-sense letter to Yuri Andropov. Former senator George Mitchell helped broker peace in Ireland. Eli Pariser continues to work to end the war in Iraq. And just up the road from our family camp in Otisfield, kids from all over the conflicted Middle East learn to relate to one another on a human level at the Seeds of Peace camp.

The message from Maine is relax, make do, make peace with your self and with others. But you have to wonder whether anyone out there is listening. Maine natives are still coming home from Afghanistan and Iraq in coffins, and war with Iran looms large and ominous on the horizon.

Every time I think about how fortunate we million are to live in Maine, what a beautiful, sensible place it is, I am troubled once again to recall that Mohammed Atta and two of his fellow 9/11 terrorists spent their last night on Earth in South Portland. The Maine Mall, of course, isn't Maine, but still you'd have thought some essential Maine goodness would have rubbed off on them, opened their eyes, their minds, their hearts.

How shocked the would-be martyrs must have been to discover that there were no virgins waiting for them in paradise, that their fate was just incineration in a jet-fuel inferno. I watched it all from rural Sedgwick where I was visiting Bill Donnell at the old mill where he makes the world's best clapboards. Alas, so close. The fools had been in paradise and just didn't realize it.

# THE ALL-AMERICAN GAME

There are two balls on the desk before me. One is a dirty white Rawlings baseball, a foul ball daughter Tess picked up at a Sea Dogs game years ago, saying, "What's this?" and flipping it away when the ball landed beside her as she played in the sand. The other is a yellow Brine lacrosse ball I picked up on one of my frequent half-time perambulations around the Yarmouth turf field while watching her play. The woods and bushes around the synthetic field are filled with errant lacrosse balls flung there by boisterous boys in light armor.

Though they are similar in size and the same in weight, the differences between a baseball and a lacrosse ball are marked, as are the merits of the two spring sports. Both baseball and lacrosse are supremely American games, the one speaking to our pastoral past, the other to our tribal ancestry. Invented by Native Americans, lacrosse has passed in recent years from its traditional strongholds in prep schools through yuppie suburbs like Cape Elizabeth and

Yarmouth, and into mainstream popularity statewide.

Around these parts, Waynflete, Cape Elizabeth, North Yarmouth Academy, and Yarmouth tend to be the "lax" powerhouses. Until lacrosse came along, Yarmouth fielded championship baseball teams. Now baseball sometimes seems like lacrosse's poor cousin. It's difficult for small schools to be competitive at both.

Last week, along with a half-dozen lost lax balls, I found a waterlogged baseball in the woods at half-time and gave it to a friend's Airedale to play with. By the time the game was over, the diligent dog had gnawed and worried the ball into a pile of chewed cowhide and soggy yarn.

At one time or another, every red-blooded American boy (and not a few girls) has deconstructed a baseball, the tightly wound little universe of which is a wonder to reveal. Nine inches in circumference and five ounces in weight, a baseball is a complex object consisting of a center pill of cork encased in rubber. Around this core are four distinct layers of wool and cotton windings, the entire sphere covered in a literal skin of cowhide, two figure-eight yin-yang halves stitched together with eighty-eight inches of waxed red thread in a hundred and eight stitches. Once made in Haiti, Rawlings baseballs are now hand-stitched in Costa Rica.

A lacrosse ball, on the other hand, is a remarkably simple object, a ball of rubber eight inches in circumference and weighing five ounces and made in China. When Native Americans invented the game, lacrosse balls were made of hair, deerskin, and knotted strips of leather, but since 1867 rubber has been the rule. As recently as the 1990s, when her oldest sister Hannah played, lacrosse sticks were still made of wood and gut, but Tess's twenty-first-century stick is a high-tech thing of plastics and graphite.

I keep the baseball around as a kind of athletic worry bead. I finger it and try out different grips while I'm watching the Red Sox on TV. My hands still seem to retain some muscle memory from when I first pitched in Little League. I'm glad to see that this year Little League Baseball finally got around to establishing pitch counts for skinny little arms. Mine used to throb and go limp after six innings of throwing as hard as I could. That throb returns to this day if I throw too many snowballs, chucking them at trees for the satisfaction of still having an accurate arm and to gauge just how much control I've lost.

These days, however, I am happiest as a spectator. I love watching the girls play lacrosse, whipping the yellow ball from stick to stick on a dead run. I even enjoy not knowing the rules very well; that way I can't get too upset at blown calls. I'm amazed though that there are any rules at all in boys' lacrosse, a sport in which beating each other with metal poles and shoving each other to the ground seems to be allowed. Boys' lacrosse is a brutal game compared to girls' lacrosse, more like hand-to-hand combat than sport, but, given their druthers, I'm pretty sure Tess and many of her teammates would just as soon don helmets and pads and go to war.

Lacrosse has gotten a bit more civilized in recent years though. When I first started watching a few years ago, there were sidelines on the field but they were not enforced. Players roamed in and out of bounds at will, apparently a residual freedom from ancient days when Native Americans played the game in unmarked fields. Now when a ball goes out of bounds it's out of bounds. That, I suppose, is progress.

I still prefer the peculiarity of the baseball with its hand-sewn seams and hidden layers to the smooth, soft, featureless rubber monolith of the lacrosse ball, but lacrosse now rules out here in the preferred suburbs.

# STRICTLY FOR THE BIRDS

Late one afternoon as the gray sky was preparing to go black and winter contemplated spring, ten mourning doves sat high in the bare branches of the maple trees next door like quarter notes on an organic staff. I doubt that anyone else in this dim world saw them, and that's too bad because I can't read music. I would love to know what a pianist might have made of them, or an organist, or perhaps even a clarinetist. The doves were surely musical even in their stillness and silence, but whether their perched arrangement notated the atonal dissonance of chaos or the lovely melody of a song beyond hearing I will never know.

In a lot of ways, last year was strictly for the birds. In human terms, "strictly for the birds" holds the negative connotation of poor quality, even worthlessness, and as far as human history goes that's probably an apt description of a year in which our failings as a species outweighed our successes. But the older I get, the less anthropocentric I become. What's happening with the birds—and for that matter, the insects, fish, and mammals—is ultimately no less important to this planet than what is happening to human beings, perhaps even more so.

We haven't seen the wild turkeys all winter, but I expect shortly they will be parading down the railroad tracks at nightfall again as usual. These big, wary, and potentially belligerent birds have made an astonishing comeback since being reintroduced to Maine in the 1970s. Wild turkey population estimates are now 20,000, roughly the same number as black bears. Never in my life have turkeys been so much in evidence. I like to think it's an environmental success story, but something in my skeptical nature make me suspect that the prevalence of wild turkeys, mourning doves, coyotes, and whitetail deer betokens a disaster in the making.

We're being visited much more frequently now by slate-colored juncos and cardinal couples, and the redwing blackbirds are back in the marsh, but the black-capped chickadees still dominate the bird feeder as they have all winter. Yesterday I clipped a few handfuls of matted fur off our old dog and tossed the clippings into the feeder tree. Within seconds the resourceful chickadees were checking it out in beaksfull. High in the trees of the surrounding woods there are now nests lined with dog hair just waiting to welcome new arrivals.

Now that the snow has begun to melt away, a desert of black oil sunflower seeds is beginning to emerge beneath the feeder. Red squirrels, gray squirrels, and mice tunneling beneath the snow from the basement feed on what the birds have dropped and I have spilled.

Every morning, after putting the coffee on for Carolyn, I scoop a quart container of seeds out of the bag in my sunroom office and carry it to the cylindrical feeder hanging from the Norway spruce Carolyn has been urging me to cut down for years. I trimmed off the lower branches a few years ago to reclaim some of the yard, but I am loath to remove a tree that the birds seem to enjoy.

Most days, as soon as I have poured the seed into the feeder, a lone sentry bird immediately broadcasts the news. Within thirty seconds, a dozen chickadees come swooping in from the woods, little black darts from the cold blue sky.

I love the chickadees' instinct to spread the good news. Squirrels chatter irritably and chase one another away, and blue jays bugle and bully their way to the feeder, but chickadees have apparently determined that it is better to share what has been provided than to fight over it. Wise birds. They deserve a more respectful name. All living things, of course, deserve more respect than we give them. Maybe this will be the year.

# YOUR HUMBLE SERVANT

In June I will be completing my second three-year term as a deacon at the First Parish Congregational Church (UCC) in Yarmouth. It has been a humbling experience for someone not known for humility and I will miss it.

In theory, the board of deacons assists the pastors with the spiritual life of the congregation, but, being a precarious Christian at best, I'm on thin theological ice when it comes to things liturgical. In reality, however, a great deal of the work of the deaconate amounts to doing chores, and I love doing chores. Arriving early to change candles, prepare communion, make coffee, turn on the sound system, post the hymn numbers, etc., and staying afterwards to wash dishes and pick up the sanctuary is right up my alley.

Most of the time, a deacon works behind the scenes, so it feels a bit disingenuous to be calling attention to myself here in print. I feel even more compromised and conspicuous in a role I helped create for the deacons as outside greeters, standing out in front of the church each Sunday morning to assist those who need help getting into the church.

Deacons are supposed to help increase the congregation by making the church as welcoming as possible though, so giving people a hand with parking, wheelchairs, and stairs seems the least we can do. Fortunately, First Parish has now undertaken a $1.3 million capital campaign designed to improve accessibility by the installation of an elevator, creation of a universal walkway, and interior renovations to make room for wheelchairs.

My conspicuous role as a church deacon alternately amuses and annoys my teenage daughter, who has the same skeptical view of organized religion that I had at her age. I tell her what my grandmother used to tell me when we'd get into discussions about religion: "You'll believe when you need to believe."

We all heed the call to worship for different reasons and at different times in our lives, and yet, ultimately, we are all more or less the same. Ashes to ashes, dust to dust. What I value most about church-going is the sense of fellowship and community. In church, we seem able to put aside our philosophical and political differences and relate to one another as human beings, fellow mortals, people trying to live a decent life in an indecent world.

I thought of this over the weekend when I served as a deacon at the funeral of a fellow congregant, a man exactly my own age, who I had first related to only as a political adversary. In fact, I once wrote some very unflattering things about him in this very column. When he began showing up in church, however, those partisan political differences no longer seemed anywhere near as important as the fact that he, like me, was looking for spiritual guidance, was a good father, a family man, and an active member of the community. We traded a few good-natured barbs from time to time, but we made peace and became sideline and Sunday morning friends. I will miss him.

Assisting at funerals has been the most meaningful part of my service as a deacon. Over the past six years, I have had a modest role in trying to make sure that everything went as smoothly as possible as we have celebrated the lives of an artist friend of mine, an athlete just out of high school, a popular local musician, a prominent local businessman, the mother of one of my daughter's classmates, and, even more painfully, that of one of her classmates. The way a community comes together in times of grief is a powerful and sustaining thing to experience. As a deacon, there are little things you can sometimes do to help make the occasion more empowering for loved ones and friends, like inviting them to ring the church bells or to extinguish the candles on the altar.

One of these days, those bells are going to toll for me and someone will extinguish my flame. In the meantime, it's good to stay busy. It's good to be of service. Being a deacon is as close to being a servant as I have ever gotten, and I have come to believe that we are never more ourselves than when we are serving others.

# I AM MY DOG

The animal control officer showed up at the back door the other day to ask me if I knew where my dog was. Unfortunately, I knew exactly where my dog was; he was up the street sticking his nose in someone else's business, a bad habit he probably picked up from me. Since I had been warned about letting my dog run at large once before (albeit ten years ago), I politely waited while the officer wrote me a ticket. Sure enough, while I was being issued a summons, old Ritz came trotting back down the street as though he were free to come and go as he pleased, which he pretty much has been for the past fifteen years. Not any longer, however.

I got Ritz for free back in the summer of 1988 from Portland furniture-maker Jamie Johnston. Ritz's mother was Jamie's standard poodle Soda and his father was rumored to have been a shepherd-husky cross just passing through town. My daughters named him after the crackers, not the hotel. In the winter, when we let his gray coat grow out, Ritz looks a lot like a sheepdog. When we clip him in the summer he can look like anything from a greyhound to Walt Disney's Tramp.

As we all know, some people grow to look like their dogs, but I *am* my dog. Not only are we both old, lame, scruffy, and gray, but we also have pretty much the same attitude, disposition, and outlook. Both our lives revolve around the mail (Ritz barks its arrival and I sort through the bills looking for checks) and meals (I sit at the table and he sits under it). We both like to lie in the sun and need a nap in the afternoon. We both love kids, but we're largely relegated these days to watching their games rather than participating. And we've both grown increasingly nervous about electrical storms as we've gotten older.

We also have a woman in common. We both love my wife more than we like each other. Carolyn is a faithful mistress, dutifully walking Ritz around the block before work each day and last thing before bedtime, doggie bag in hand. She would never just open the door when Ritz scratches and let him out, as I sometimes do. I'm sure she was disappointed in both of us for running afoul of the law, me for being so lazy and Ritz for being such an incorrigible trash hound. The last time I had to take him to the vet the diagnosis was "dietary indiscretion." Tinfoil is tough on the digestive system.

I guess you could say Ritz and I are both troublemakers in our own ways. He'll poop on your lawn and he'll get into your trash if you're thoughtless enough to leave it outside. I'll tell you what I think whether you want to hear it or not. But it's also true that our barks are worse than our bites. As far as I know, Ritz has never bitten anyone in his fifteen years on Earth, unless you count a few little nips he's given me when I've tried to clip his paws. Neither of us likes having our hair cut or our feet touched.

We both get along just fine with people we don't really care for and Ritz even gets along with cats. Back in his cat-chasing days, he'd only chase cats that would run from him. If they stood their ground, he'd lose interest. If they hissed or spat at him, he'd hightail it. I used to be pretty much the same way before I got married and settled down.

Ritz and I were both fast and light in our day, but neither of us does much running anymore. When he was young, I'd take him in the car with me wherever I went and when we returned I'd drop him off at the top of the street and let him race the car home. For years he would beat me home easily. Then it got to be closer to a tie. When I started beating him into the driveway four or five years ago, I knew he was getting old.

These days I don't take Ritz with me in the car because he's not always in control of his bodily functions, but if I did drop him off at the top of the street I'm not sure he'd bother to come straight home. He'd probably poke around in someone's yard in search of good smells or free eats and I'd end up with another summons. Which is as it should be. It's both illegal and not very neighborly to let your dog run loose. Still, I look at all my neighbors a little differently now, knowing that one of them called the police instead of calling me.

## LET SLEEPING DOGS LIE

When I was growing up we had almost as many dogs as we had houses. Well, not quite actually. By the time I was twelve, we had moved seventeen times, but we had only owned about six dogs.

Princess, a regal tri-colored collie, was my totem childhood pet. She refused to allow anyone she didn't know or didn't like into the yard, ran afoul of the mailman, and had to be sent to a farm (at least that's what I was told). Then there was Rip, the collie who replaced Princess. I don't recall what happened to him. Probably a victim of one of our frequent moves. RIP, Rip.

After the pedigreed collies, we had a succession of all-American mutts, each one about the size of an overweight beagle—Sootie, Heidi, and Cokie. Sootie had a litter of pups in my bed. That's the only way I have of distinguishing the three bitches in my memory. Finally, there was the full-grown boxer we adopted, but he didn't stick around long enough for his name to register. The first week we had him, we left him alone for a day and came home to a houseful of torn curtains and overturned houseplants. Apparently, the boxer was savvy enough to realize he had been adopted by a family of inept dog lovers.

Some, if not all, of these dogs very likely had to be "put to sleep," though their exits from our young lives were always quick, unexpected, and unceremonious. I assume Dad must have taken care of the dirty work. We just shed our tears after the fact. Well into my teens, I could make myself cry at will just by thinking about Princess—a reservoir of emotion that came in handy for acting in plays and breaking up with girlfriends.

Now I'm dad and I just can't bring myself to do it. As though in reaction against my peripatetic childhood and cavalier canine history, I have owned just one house and just one dog. Ritz will turn eighteen in June. The little girls I got him for have both graduated from college and he is older than our youngest daughter by three years. The vet started offering to "put him down" for me almost two years ago. His eyesight is failing. He can barely hear. His hindquarters sag to the floor if he stands in one place. He has to be carried down stairs. He can't control his bowels or his bladder. And unless he manages to lie down smack in the middle of the blanket-covered throw rug at the foot of our bed, he can't get up without help. His feet go out from under him, he pants and grunts, gives up, and just does his business where he lies.

I thought I'd know when it was time to have him put to sleep, but he's not making it easy. I thought it would be obvious when he was suffering, making euthanasia an act of compassion. But damn, even in his infirm and unsanitary state, Ritz still takes a profound interest in his (or anyone else's) food, still likes to sniff around the edges of his rapidly diminishing world, and still enjoys lying in the sun on the front lawn and watching the world go by. I can't deny him that.

To be perfectly honest, I keep hoping I'll wake up one morning and old Ritz will have expired quietly in the night, but the vet tells me a dog's heart will just go on beating indefinitely. It's his muscles that give out. So I've got this smelly bag of bones sleeping at the foot of my bed, soiling my house, stinking the place up, and waking me at all hours of the night with the indignity of his bodily needs. The fact that I can't seem to bring myself to end his life has something to do, of course, with the fact that I love him. But I keep wondering whether my tenderhearted lack of resolve is ultimately about sparing him or just about sparing me.

# AMONG THE MISSING

There are places all around Greater Portland that have
strong personal associations for me, places that always make
me think of people I miss. This occurred to me last Saturday
when Carolyn and I took daughter Tess and our old dog
Ritz out for a spring walk on Scarborough Beach.

Scarborough Beach is my favorite place in all the world.
There were summers past when I spent every sunny day on
the sands and in the surf there, but this day the beach was
still in its winter condition, steep, narrow, roaring surf, flot-
sam and jetsam washed way back into the dune grass.
Precious little sea glass to be found.

Whenever I go to Scarborough Beach I think of Gary
Merrill. When Gary was living down on the lanes at Prouts
Neck, we used to park at his cottage and stop in for a quick
visit. I admired Gary greatly, not so much as a great actor
and movie star (which he had been), but as a self-proclaimed
beach bum who had seen through the hollowness of celebrity
and had chosen to live out his life modestly back in his native

Maine. Things were better when Gary was still was around. I also think of my old friend artist Chip Chadbourn when I go to the beach. I pass his former home and studio in Yarmouth almost daily, but somehow I associate Chip more strongly with the beach. He was a compleat sensualist, in love with the sun, good food and drink, painting, and the beauty of Maine right up until the end. Chip was the first serious artist I ever met and it was a painting he had done of sunbathers on a beach that first awakened my interest in art.

As it happens, I trace my passion for writing and literature to another beach dweller—my freshman English teacher at Westbrook High School. Altie Hayden lived at Higgins Beach and I used to park my motor scooter in her yard back in the 1960s when Higgins Beach was more popular with teenagers than Scarborough Beach. Mrs. Hayden's love of literature transcended prescribed curricula and made me realize that writing was a vital and ongoing enterprise, not just something done by the long-dead white men to confound students.

When we head home from the beach, we often make a detour south on Route One to get ice cream at Len Libby's, and whenever I pass the entrance to Scarborough Downs I think of Joe Ricci, outlaw capitalist, angry young man, and anti-authoritarian crusader. I miss Joe because he never backed down from a good fight and he was usually right.

If we come home by way of Portland, we come over the Casco Bay Bridge and head up High Street past the former home and bookshop of Francis O'Brien, bookman extraordinaire, antiquarian and the soul of Portland. When Francis died, a good deal of Portland's memory and history died with him. I think of Francis often, because I often have questions only he could have answered.

Finally, when we cross into Falmouth, whether out on I-295 or over Martin's Point Bridge, I look right to see the fine white house where my maternal grandparents, Paul and Mildred Gibson, used to live and where my mother and I passed much of the Korean War while my father was away in the navy. The house overlooks the causeway to Macworth Island and my grandfather, who was dying of cancer at the time, would look out the window and tell me stories he made up about the rabbits that came out to play on the causeway at night.

Bampi Gibson also taught me songs that, at two and three years old, I would sing for his friends when they came to visit, songs like "I Went to the Animal Fair" which conjured an image that has stayed with me to this day—"The old baboon by the light of the moon was combing his auburn hair."

Whoever lives in that fine white house today can have no idea that they inhabit my past any more than I am aware of the life that was lived in my house before I bought it almost thirty years ago now. I don't think of myself as a particularly nostalgic person, but the older I get the more I am aware that we all carry the past around with us as we wander into an uncertain future.

## JUST A DOG

A few hours ago I finally did my duty as a pet owner and had our old dog Ritz put down. Had he lived another few weeks, he would have been eighteen, but I had been dragging my heels for months as his infirmities became more and more pronounced, so finally Carolyn made the appointment and we went together to see him off.

We were both in tears as we led Ritz into the examining room where the vet administered the lethal dose. Ritz accepted his fate calmly and with dignity. He didn't whimper or cry or even try to get away. As the veterinarian injected him in the right front leg, he simply relaxed, put his head on Carolyn and died peacefully in her arms. If I can muster half as much grace and courage when my time comes, I will die a happy man.

At the risk of getting too maudlin, I will confess that I am in tears as I write this. Old Ritz was a sweetheart and I loved him very much. I don't want this to become a eulogy for a dog, but it is true that in his long lifetime Ritz never harmed a living thing. Oh, he did tree his quota of cats and he occasionally made a mess of the neighbors' trash, but, hey, I've done worse. I keep thinking, in fact, that a fitting way to celebrate his passing from our lives would be for me to sneak out early some morning and strew a little trash around the neighborhood.

For some reason, I wasn't expecting such a sense of emptiness and loss. Sure, Ritz had been part of the family since our older daughters, both now college graduates, were in kindergarten or first grade, but he was just a dog, right? Wrong.

I realize now how callous it was of me not long ago to ask a neighbor who had just put his family dog down whether they were planning to get another dog. When I remarked to Carolyn that we could get a puppy, her answer was swift and forthright. "We don't want a puppy." And when we do decide to get another dog, some puppy-to-be-named-later will have some pretty big paws to fill.

What is it about dogs that moves me so? I have had friends and relatives die without crying nearly as much as I have cried over Ritz. Come to think of it, the only movie I ever cried at was *Old Yeller.* I'm just a sucker when it comes to canines I guess. I think it must have something to do with their loyalty, the vaunted fidelity of Fido. Or maybe it's the faith they place in us. Did I keep that faith or betray it when I decided it was time to end his life?

I suppose the anthropocentric view would be that dogs lack self-consciousness and therefore have no sense of their own mortality. So I was just projecting my own mortal dread upon old Ritz when I saw the stoicism with which he accepted his own end. But we're talking about an animal who could sense Carolyn approaching three miles away, who read the daily news on the wind, who knew from the timbre of your voice whether you were putting him in the car to take him to the lake or to the kennel. So don't tell me he didn't know. He knew.

I don't know whether dogs have souls, but if they do, Ritz had a good soul. And if dogs don't have souls, I don't know why not. Sleep well, sweet boy. We loved you, so you broke our hearts.

# A WALK IN THE PARK

On a chilled, sunny afternoon last week, I took a brisk walk through Yarmouth's Royal River Park just to get my blood flowing again. The muddy Royal was pouring along its iced, leafless banks on its way to the Lower Falls and the distant sea beyond.

With the exception of a couple of solitary dog walkers, I had the asphalt path along the river all to myself.

The Lenten season is a sad yet hopeful time, and that was the mood I was in as I strode along the river, trying to match my steps to my heartbeats. But I wasn't thinking of *the* Resurrection as much as I was of the chances of resurrecting optimism in a country and a culture that has slipped so far from life, liberty, and the pursuit of happiness. Nature and culture both move in predictable cycles, not necessarily making progress, just changing and renewing. But are we now so far off the track, I wonder, that we won't be able to swing back?

It is now apparent to most of us that the violent conservative lurch to the right has done more damage to our country in a decade than the liberal swing to the left did in the 1960s and 1970s. We can only hope that we will be able to undo all of the harm to our environment, education, economy, prestige, and self-image during the inevitable liberal backlash.

We liberals always want to make sure everyone is taken care of, while conservatives seem to want everyone to take care of themselves. I'm as liberal as they come, but I don't know about you; all this polarizing radicalism in American society has made me hungry for some good old-fashioned moderation.

I'd like to see progressives embrace some new energy sources, for instance. If we're not going to drill for oil in the Arctic, build more nuclear power plants, and erect more dams (and I trust we are not), then we have to actively develop renewable energy sources such as wind and solar power. And I'd like to see conservatives acknowledge that serious energy conservation has to be the cornerstone of a national energy policy.

Even as I was enjoying the sunny, snowless March day, I was worrying that this moderate winter was a foreshadowing of things to come, a time in the not-too-distant future when Maine winters will be as moderate as those in Richmond, Virginia, today. If so, say good-bye to ski resorts and snowmobiles.

Things are definitely out of whack. And it's not just the environment, it's foreign policy, it's the media, it's education, and it's the economy. Even locally you can see what happens when people tilt too far to one side. Just look at Portland, a proud liberal city, but one that teeters back and forth between economic development and growth management so precariously that it drives business and development away.

Now I'm told that my hometown of Westbrook is becoming the new Portland, a small city open to dynamic new possibilities. Of course, when I was growing up there in the 1960s, Westbrook was S. D. Warren and nothing else. Rival schools chanted at us, "Go back! Go back! Go back to the mill!" Today, there is a residual SAPPI paper mill, but, with the paper industry in Maine in its death throes, I have to wonder how long they will still be making paper in the Paper City.

Yarmouth, too, was once a paper-mill town. The old Forest Paper Company straddled the Royal the way SAPPI does the Presumpscot. In its day, Forest Paper was a great innovator, pioneering the switch from rag to wood fiber for making paper. But the mill closed in 1923 and burned to the ground in 1931. Today, a century of human industry and lifetimes of work have been reduced to piles of brick rubble in the underbrush along the Royal River Park footpath. Striding past these industrial remains on my way back to the car just reinforced the sense that I was walking through the ruins of time.

1956

# THE MOTHER OF ALL COLUMNS

Mother's Day, which has been observed the second Sunday in May since 1914, has always struck me as a conspiracy by the nation's florists to peddle more flowers. We shouldn't need a designated day to celebrate motherhood. Every day should be Mother's Day, keeping us mindful that it was Mother who brought us into the world and gave us life.

This Mother's Day, however, does provide a logical occasion for me to address a longstanding failure on my part—the failure of a scribbling fool to devote so much as a word to his own dear mom. I wish I could say this was an oversight, but, in fact, I have knowingly and assiduously avoided dragging Mom into print lo these many years. Lord knows I have been more than willing to discuss all but the most tender aspects of my own life in print and, at one time or another, have essayed my dad, my lovely wife and beautiful daughters, my grandparents and my younger brothers, but I have always avoided writing anything about Mom. Why is a delicate matter.

I wouldn't be writing about my mother now, in fact, had not the embargo on Mom columns gone on so long that it has become conspicuous. Geezum, why doesn't Eddie ever write anything about Mom? Doesn't he love his mother? Does he have maternal "issues" he can't deal with? Is there just nothing worth saying about Mom? None of the above.

I have not written about my mother over the years primarily because I am afraid I might unwittingly upset her. And it's not that I would have anything critical or unflattering to say, it's just that Betty Beem tends to take things to heart. I could say just about anything truthful about Al Beem and be confident that old Dad would laugh it off, but even in this column, which is meant as a son's heartfelt declaration of love and appreciation for his mother, I fear I will say something that will unintentionally hurt Mom's feelings. In fact, I may already have done so.

The relationship of a boy to his mother is a powerful and defining force. I may bear my father's name, but I am my mother's son. Dad, who spent long stretches of his life away in the navy and the merchant marine, likes to say facetiously that "The boys are the products of my heredity and their mother's environment—I was never around." That's not an entirely true statement of course, but there is truth in it.

I have long regarded my father as the moon and my mother as the sun. With Dad there was a side you never saw, not a dark side, just the non-family side, the years at sea, his working life. With Mom there was just a total, warm and all-encompassing presence. If she had a life of her own while we three boys were growing up, I don't know what it was. She seemed to exist for us alone. If I had problems or got in trouble, Dad could remain so reasonable and detached that I sometimes wondered whether he really cared (which, of course, he did), but it was pretty obvious that Mom suffered every pain, disappointment, and worry with me. She was like an extension of myself—or I of her. It's that maternal sensitivity I fear offending.

Because she had always been a twenty-four-hour-a-day mother, it took me awhile after I left the nest to appreciate that Mom did have a life and interests of her own. For one thing, as I was growing up in the 1950s and 1960s, she was one of the few mothers who had graduated from college—both Westbrook Junior College and Lesley College. She had had a career as a nursery school teacher before marrying and raising a family. Once her boys were grown, she embarked on a belated career as a real estate agent, becoming, as we often kid her, her own best client. Dad's shore jobs may have dragged us all over Maine and New England, seventeen addresses between 1949 and 1960 when we finally settled in Westbrook, but at last count Mom had relocated in Westbrook seven times, not to mention brief stays in Portland and Falmouth.

The most important thing I learned from my mother is unconditional love. She always told us that there was nothing in this world we could not tell her. I believed her, because it was true. I have tried to teach the same thing to my daughters. Candor is a priceless gift. So with that in mind, I figure it's high time I say in public something I have said fifty-odd years in private. I love you, Mom. Happy Mother's Day.

# IN PRAISE OF TRANSPLANTS

When our daughter Hannah was home over Memorial Day weekend, she dug up some lilies of the valley from outside her bedroom window and took them, along with a clump of forget-me-nots, back to Providence to plant outside her new apartment. Seeing her poaching plants from her mother's garden made me smile to think how much her mother's daughter she is becoming.

It wasn't all that long ago that I watched Carolyn digging up rhubarb from her mother's yard in Portland to transplant here in Yarmouth. Come to think of it, while she was home, Hannah made a deep-dish peach-rhubarb pie from her grandmother's transplanted rhubarb.

The practice of sharing plants strikes me as one of the loveliest customs of a civil society, creating as it does an organic bond between family members and friends. Our modest little yard, in fact, is full of things green and growing that arrived as transplants from the gardens of others.

We owe our little raspberry patch to our good neighbor

Bob Robson. The jack-in-the-pulpits below my office window came from Carolyn's mother's garden, but they started from plants her brother's earth science teacher gave him back in the 1960s. The irises, which are my favorite flowers, came from Carolyn's sister Janice's yard. The coreopsis came from across town in the yard of our friend Carol Greenlaw. Sally Ward, a master gardener now alas moving from Yarmouth to Brunswick, gave Carolyn both the lady's mantle and a small hemlock tree now growing in the back yard. The hostas growing all around the house came from Colleen Snyder's yard in Scarborough. The purple trillium under the huge white pine, the glory of our little suburban estate, came from my own mother's woodsy yard in Westbrook. And the dahlias grew from bulbs we got at church when a green-thumbed member, Bob Walker, I believe, thinned his garden and brought armloads of bulbs in to share.

Plants from family and friends are the most meaningful transplants, but Carolyn delights in anything free, so she is still quite pleased with the orange azalea bush that we picked up on the side of Middle Road in Cumberland a few years ago. The prior owners were obviously landscaping and had put the bush out on the roadside with a "Free" sign on it.

Of course, plants are not the only free material gracing our little yard. Here and there, you'll find the odd granite block lifted from Vinalhaven and beach stones from up and down the coast. In fact, the yard itself is pretty much donated, the back half consisting of spring street sweepings courtesy of the local public works department and mulch carted home year after year from the municipal compost pile at the dump (I mean, the transfer station).

This redistribution of flora, fill, and fertilizer is a good thing. It helps keep us grounded. Frankly, I'm not much of a gardener myself, but I do love to walk around the yard and watch what is growing and what is going on. Carolyn, who tends to the garden barefoot, urges me to take my shoes off when I make my inspections, feeling that I have a tendency to be too cerebral and not in touch enough with the earth. She may have a point. But then sooner or later we all return to earth. And the only afterlife I can imagine, the only immortality I desire, is to add my atoms to the wondrous profusion of nature, the only earthly riches that count, the green life we pass down and pass around.

# THE ETHICAL DILEMMAS OF YARD WORK

In a neat bit of environmental exchange, the town crew last week picked up a winter's worth of fallen limbs and branches which will eventually be returned to us in the form of free mulch. This year, however, what with the old pickup truck having died in Rhode Island, I had no way to cart the free mulch home, so I had the local nursery deliver three yards of compost which came from the Auburn recycling center. I figured that screened and delivered it was well worth twenty-four dollars a yard.

My beautiful, barefoot wife loves dirt, manure, compost, and mulch. She says it's the Polish peasant in her, but I tend to think it's also the little girl making mud pies in her that explains her affection for soil. In any event, she wasted no time in spreading the steamy black stinking rot all over her flower beds.

The nurseryman told me he had been selling a ton of compost this spring but not much mulch at all. He wondered whether something had been written about mulch that he hadn't seen. There sure had. The environmental group Waterkeepers Alliance is leading an anti-cypress-mulch campaign that featured a full-page ad in the *New York Times* a few weeks ago that asked, "Why kill a tree to grow a flower?"

It seems that renegade loggers are denuding cypress swamps in the Louisiana bayou in order to grind the trees up for garden mulch. So if your gardens are neatly trimmed with cypress mulch, you're partially responsible for Hurricane Katrina flooding the Gulf Coast. I'm being a bit facetious, of course, but some communities in Florida have gone so far as to ban cypress mulch after seeing what the mulch industry has done to its coastal wetlands. Ashes to ashes, bark to mulch.

Several of my neighbors have been having large trees removed from their yards this spring. The neighborhood looks a bit more naked for it, but I suppose a homeowner has a right to a little afternoon sunshine, not to mention the right to protect the house from falling limbs. Now, however, my beautiful, barefoot wife wants me to chop down a tree in our yard. Over my dead body! (Which is probably what it would be if I tried to chop down a tree.)

The tree in question is a Norway spruce that was only slightly taller than me when we moved here almost thirty years ago. Now it's thirty feet tall and I expect its roots to burst through into the basement any day. If I hadn't limbed it up to a height of seven feet a few years ago to reclaim some the back yard, the bottom limbs would be brushing the house. The reason I staunchly defend it is that it is "the bird tree."

The bird tree stands right outside the kitchen window

and an extraordinary array of birds flock to the feeder filled with black oil sunflower seeds. Just today, I have seen the gang of chickadees that think they own it as well as nuthatches, cardinals, blue jays, grackles, redwing blackbirds, a tufted titmouse, and sundry confusing spring warblers, one of whom knocked himself silly yesterday trying to fly through the glass door into my sun-porch office to see what I was writing.

I have a big owl cutout on the door to prevent just such an eventuality, but for an hour or so every morning the sun seems to hit the door just right so that it reflects the bird tree and probably looks like an escape route to winged beings. We've had three or four bird strikes this spring but only one fatality. So maybe I should cut down the bird tree after all—as a public service to the birds.

We've only got a third of an acre down here at the bottom of the street, but I can't imagine how folks with much more land manage to look after it, let alone deal with all of the ethical dilemmas that come with yard work.

I have resolved the lawn-mowing dilemma to my satisfaction. Rather than replace the last in a long line of cheap, hard-to-start power mowers with yet another clunker, I finally broke down and purchased an old-fashioned non-motorized reel mower. The lawn doesn't have that uniformly manicured look any more and I have to mow constantly to stay ahead of the growth, but I feel good knowing that I'm no longer contributing to pollution—at least not with my lawnmower. If my lawn were any bigger, mowing would become a full-time job, but then, as a general rule of thumb, if your lawn is big enough that you think you need a riding mower, you've definitely got too much lawn.

# SUMMER

## THE NEIGHBORHOOD
## A PERSONAL GEOGRAPHY

My back yard was once a bog. The sump pump droning away in the cellar all spring is a seasonal reminder that my little house stands on filled wetlands. Fifty years ago and more, bulldozers scraped off some fifteen feet of sandy soil and woods from up the street and deposited it—roots, stumps, and all—on my lot. Today, my lot still falls gently away from the house into a patch of swamp alders and then into a drainage ditch that separates my property from the railroad tracks and the deer-and-coyote-infested woods beyond.

The street where I live was the town's first subdivision, unless, of course, you count the original "division of the lots" in 1727, which apportioned the town into ten-acre tracts to the first settlers. When our street was laid out in 1955–56 there were no subdivision ordinances in place, thus the street took shape as a one-third mile-loop of forty-five capes and ranches on 100 x 100-foot lots. This cramped, uninspired egg-crate design was saved from total uniformity by a few oversize odd lots at the bottom of the loop and the fact that the whole development was poorly surveyed at best.

Surveying irregularities, I am told, account for the slight jog left the roadway takes at the top of the street and the little public esplanade across the street from my house. All the kids in the neighborhood play there and the town mows the grass, so I don't really mind the error. Nor do I mind the fact that, because of poor planning on someone's part, my single-family cape shared a street number (30A & 30B) with one half of the duplex next door until a few years ago when Enhanced 9-1-1 required the renumbering of the entire town and we were anointed 130.

It was only recently, however, that I realized that my street is exactly the sort of over-intensive, ill-considered, ticky-tacky sort of development planners and environmentalists counseled Maine communities to avoid for many years. Of course, it also happens to be a wonderful place to live.

One of the primary reasons our neighborhood works is that despite its density (an attribute touted as a good thing in the years since this essay was originally published in 1990), it has a rural feel to it. To begin with, there are now sidewalks and there is no center stripe on the street. Being neither throughway nor dead end but a loop, there is not much traffic and children play safely in the street. The level of street lighting is low. The developers, if they did nothing else right, had the good sense to leave mature trees standing throughout. And now that the street is more than fifty years old, the big pine, elm, spruce, and maple trees have been joined by all manner of ornamental shrubs, bushes, and trees to create a lush and leafy little landscape, in my case verging on overgrown.

This street of big trees and small houses is, in some ways, an extension of myself into the world. Head, heart, body, room, home, yard, street, neighborhood, town, etc. What I comprehend as my neighborhood is, in fact, a simple quadrilateral bounded by this street, the main road off which it runs, a side road paralleling this one, and the railroad tracks that run behind my house. The territory thus enclosed is an area of perhaps sixty-five acres within which there are sixty-five homes, a sand pit, a twenty-acre wood, three frog ponds, and two little brick schoolhouses (now landscape and investment offices) where my two older daughters attended kindergarten. I occasionally trek downtown to the library, the post office, the corner store, or the church, but these few circumscribed acres are my real walking world.

*Gossip*

I have made all this mine over the past twenty-six years, but my grasp of the landscape is tenuous compared to that of the great lady who lived out her life in the bog house at the head of the street. Elizabeth Barker Murphy has passed on now, but she lived in the house where she was born, an Italianate manse built by her grandfather in 1860. Her grandfather, a sea captain, went down with his ship off California in 1867. The home he left behind is now hidden behind a wrought-iron fence and a row of high cedar.

Where my auditory cue to the neighborhood is the sound of the neighbor's bug zapper, Mrs. Murphy, a member of our church choir into her eighties or nineties, had a more musical memory. She once told me of learning to harmonize sitting on the stone wall down the road. Of waking up to the sound of the milkman's cart and sleigh bells on a winter's morn.

"It was all very pleasant," she said.

Back then there were still working farms along the main road. Mrs. Anderson over at Red Top Farm used to call this stretch of road Pound Hill, because of the cattle pound that once stood where schoolchildren now gather to wait for the bus. It was also known as Poverty Ridge, because of the mean little houses where the paper mill workers and their big families lived. The paper mill closed in 1933. A few brick remnants of it still remain in the park along the Royal River.

Mrs. Murphy, a bright and lively lady, remembered for me when my street was nothing but woods and swamp. Ninety years ago now, she and her friends used to go birch-bending in the spring, climbing birch trees and bending them over in order to bounce high into the air. The peaceful stand of pasture pine through which I sometimes walk was pastureland then. There were blueberries, too. And a spring surrounded by a wild garden of blue flag. There was a wooden barrel sunk into the spring and a tin cup for drinking. If that spring barrel still exists, it is buried under a foot of forest duff and pine needles. The tall trees whisper and creak overhead where once the pasture lay.

"Those trees," Mrs. Murphy told me, "must be about the same age as my daughter. When she was a baby all this land was excellent blueberry country."

The land where my street now stands is on the western edge of town and it remained undeveloped until after the Korean War, when the man who owned it, a ham radio operator who lived with his mother and ran a small electronics store in the village, sold it to a pair of local builders who were destined to become the town's biggest developers.

And they cut their teeth on our street.

"We were all horrified," a native of the town, now one of my neighbors, told me. "Here was this Rabbit Valley being developed with terrible little hovels."

Rabbit Valley, Fertile Valley, Pregnant Gulch: those were the names popularly assigned to the subdivision in the late 1950s and early 1960s when the first families moved in and began populating the area. The little expandable capes and ranches began selling in 1956–57 at prices ranging from $7,200 to $9,400 and, in lieu of the $500 down payment, homebuyers could put up the sweat equity of landscaping their lots and painting their houses.

"These have been great starter homes for young couples over the years," another of my neighbors, a man who bought his house in 1961 for $10,500, told me a few years after we moved in. "I never thought we'd be here twenty-nine years." He and his wife have been here now for forty-seven years.

As he reckoned it, in 1961 the average working man was making about $100 a week, $5,000 a year. The cost of a modest home was about twice your annual income. In 1982, when we bought our house for $45,000 with the help of a Farmer's Home Administration loan, I was making about $20,000, still a factor of two. In 2008 houses on the street sell for around $200,000, some with improvements for considerably more. By my reckoning, that's four times my annual income, almost twice our annual household income, and an even greater stretch for young families just starting out. To purchase a more substantial home in town would cost us at least $350,000, so we stay put.

Both husband and wife work in most of the families on the block, but dual incomes only mean staying even in today's economy. Dual incomes also mean a distinct change in the character of the neighborhood.

"Back then mothers didn't work," was a phrase I heard repeated verbatim when I talked to longtime and former residents of my street about the changes that had occurred over the years. In the beginning, virtually every house was owned by a young couple with children. At one point in the 1960s there were eighty-nine children on the street. Ten of the thirty Junior Chamber of Commerce members lived on the street. Mothers didn't work. Few people had second cars. So the young mothers stayed home, paraded around the block with baby carriages, and talked among themselves. Everyone in Fertile Valley knew everyone else and everyone's business.

Not so today. Only one or two of the forty-five homes is still inhabited by its original owner. There are still a few young mothers on the block and not all mothers work, but there are also single people, single parents, retirees, couples without children, and empty-nesters. What this mix means is that I only have a nodding acquaintance with a lot of people on the street. There are people who live within shouting distance of me whose names I do not know. I would not recognize some of my neighbors if I ran into them in the grocery store. I have only been inside five of the homes on my block, including my own, and I don't believe this is unusual.

One evening back in 1990, I sat in the kitchen of a neighbor, a man who had lived on the street since 1958. With a 1964 street directory open before him, he proceeded to give me one-line biographies of most of the people in the old neighborhood. This man had been hit by a bus. This guy was gunned down in a barroom. This guy ran out on his wife and kids. This man made a fortune in the insurance business, etc. There were tales of death and madness, infidelity and insolvency, drinking problems and marital woes. But more than anything else there were stories of lives that had just drifted on, people who had moved away or just elsewhere in town. There were even a couple of neighborhood reunions some years back, but none are planned in the near future.

Walking home that evening, I took the long way around the block, enjoying the warm summer night and the fact that every front door on the street seemed to be open. Walking slowly and trying not to be too obvious about my voyeurism, I looked in on my neighbors' lives. I fell asleep that night with a comfortable sense of how, despite the disturbances and disasters that punctuate the telling of our lives, we somehow manage to maintain the ongoing illusion of calm, normalcy, stability. I awoke the next morning to one of those warm, dry, breezy August days that is well-being incarnate.

*A walk in the woods*
"Hell, they'll never build behind me," my neighbor the gossip had thought. And for a decade or more, he had been right. Then one day in the early 1970s a bulldozer showed up in the woods out back to make way for a new street and thirty-four new homes.

The pot-bellied Irishman who developed my street went on to build as many as a thousand new homes in town before he retired and turned the business over to a son-in-law, another eager beaver who now builds subdivisions containing $400,000 executive homes. Since I moved to town in

1982, suburbia has marched steadily out to the edge of town, new streets and new developments being punched into the woods almost annually until we've run out of land. Land-use planning, zoning, sewer systems, schools, and tax burdens, however, are not the stuff of which our lives are made or lived.

On that high August morning, it was good to step into the cool, buggy green of the neighborly woods. Access to the rooted path through the pasture pine behind the ship captain's granddaughter's home is from a cul de sac halfway up the street, which suggests that someone once envisioned pushing the street right on through the woods and into the sand pit. The whole neighborhood goes sliding at the sand pit in winter and the path is always well-packed and trodden in the snow. I tend to feel slightly criminal, however, slipping into the woods on a summer's day. Were it not for the dog bounding ahead of me with his tongue hanging out, I would not feel justified in trespassing here at all. Dogs and children give one entrance.

The sand and gravel pit that lies across the piney wood is a ten-acre parcel mined years ago to provide a roadbed for Interstate 95 and left dug out and deserted ever since. The sandy bowl is now sprouting oases of weed and poplar, but the landscape is still open enough to afford excellent coasting in the winter. Near where the twenty-acre wood gives out onto the ten-acre sand pit stands a gnarled and twisted landmark maple, its core pared out and bits of rusted barbed wire at its base testifying to the former pastoral purposes of the land.

The woods and sand pit were purchased years ago by a prominent local attorney whose big house on the main road backed up to it. Having heard rumors of condominiums, the resourceful attorney exercised the power of purchase to keep the parcel from being developed and to preserve it as a recreation spot. The lawyer's daughter, who went on to become a nationally ranked ice dancer, learned to skate on the little frog pond at the back of the sand pit.

The public has used the sand pit and woods freely now for many years. The town's public access and recreation committee identified the sand pit (but somehow not the woods) as a site the town should consider acquiring, but it hasn't happened yet.

As I walked home through the woods, my shoes filled with my neighbor's sand, I found myself thinking, "Hell, they'll never build behind me," and wondering how my little world would change if they ever did.

(Updated from *Maine Times,* August 10, 1990.)

## A MILLION IS THE NEW
## HUNDRED GRAND

Each month when *Down East* magazine arrives in the mail, I
spend part of an evening engaged in a time-honored Maine
pastime—perusing the real estate ads in the back in search of
my dream house. I don't want much. A little cottage by the
sea would do. Maybe even a cabin on a lake. Just a place on
the water with character and charm, a sense of history, close
to nature, but not too far from civilization. That's the universal Maine daydream, right?

But, holy jumpin' property tax, who can afford the kind
of money they're asking for homes in Maine these days!?
Without doing the math, I'd say the average house in the
"Homes Down East" section costs between $500,000 and
$1,000,000. And there's a ton of them on the market, so
either a lot of homeowners are about to get rich or a lot of
rich folks are buying homes along the coast. Possibly both.

Not having purchased a home since 1982, I go into
sticker shock when I see what houses are selling for now. My

frame of reference is still in the tens of thousands, not the hundreds of thousands, certainly not the millions.

In 1960, when my folks purchased their first home in Westbrook, they paid $14,500 for it. When we purchased our home in Yarmouth in 1982, we paid around $40,000. Most of the modest little houses on our street that have gone on the market in the past year have sold for around $250,000. Of course this windfall won't do me a bit of good if I want to trade up in Yarmouth.

I mean, who would have believed that a quarter million dollars would ever be considered "affordable" housing? But then that's the thing about local yokels like myself who don't get out much; we don't realize the relative value of things and how the real estate markets in places like Boston and New York make Maine *look* so affordable.

Shortly before we bought our house in 1982, the Portland row house where we were renting an apartment was sold for $100,000. I remember thinking at the time that the poor out-of-state schmuck who bought it had been taken to the cleaners. Well, a lot of Maine natives have thought the same thing when they unloaded the family farm to some flatlander for what seemed a princely sum. A few years down the road, of course, that old homestead (with a bit of a makeover and a lot of marketing) fetched a king's ransom.

These days, a million is the new hundred grand. Million-dollar homes in Maine are now as common as crackers—and they're not even mansions. I mean $1.15 million might buy you a big new pre-fab on the Bagaduce River in Penobsot or a condo on Scarborough Beach, but if you want a real Maine dream house, you're talking *serious* money. How about $10,765,000 for Hidden Court in Cape Elizabeth? A magnificent, one-of-a-kind manor on fifty-two shorefront acres. Worth every penny of $10 mill I'm sure, but, lords-a-leapin', where does it end?

The quick answer, of course, is "It doesn't." Real estate is the source of most wealth in America. Land and buildings just keep appreciating. I wish I had appreciated that fact when I could have bought any building in the Old Port for $10,000.

There is a tendency to think that all the good deals, the steals, have been gobbled up. We Mainers have an "I shoulda bought it when I saw it at Marden's" mentality. But if you buy a half-million-dollar house in 2008, you'll be laughing all the way to the bank in 2028 when some fool pays you $1.5 million for it. The real estate market is constantly expanding. It's never too late to get in.

And if you don't happen to have the wherewithal to afford a $500,000 home (anymore than I could have afforded a $10,000 building in 1966), do not despair. You just have to look farther afield and wait for the population to catch up with you. You can still by a house in Millinocket or Machias for under $200,000. Personally, I've got my eye on a sweet little house for $199,500. Three bedrooms, quiet study, attached barn, two in-town acres. Sounds perfect. Now I just have to decide whether I'm willing to move to Farmington.

# ED, AL, AND EDDIE

There have been three Edgar Allen Beems. The first Edgar
Allen Beem, known as Ed, was my grandfather. Edgar Allen
Beem, Jr., who goes by Allen or Al, is my dad. I am Edgar
Allen Beem III—Ed or Edgar to most people, still Eddie to
some members of my family and a handful of old friends.
I'm sure I must have explained this all before, but as Father's
Day approaches, I've been thinking again about how differ-
ently the three of us experienced fatherhood.

Ed Beem passed away in 1971, but if he were alive today
(which I suppose is still statistically possible) he would be a
hundred and twelve. My dad is eighty-four. I am fifty-nine.
In one of the few photographs I have of the three of us
together, my grandfather is just one year older than I am
today.

The deckled-edge black-and-white snapshot, taken in
May of 1952, shows my grandfather, my grandmother, my
father, and me, all standing in front of an old Ford sedan
with the playing fields along Ludlow Street and Deering

High School in the background. A handwritten note on the back reads, "All Beems, hunh?"

In the photograph, my grandfather, who looked for all the world like the Indian chief on the nickel, is wearing a woolen athletic warm-up jacket with high-waisted, pleated slacks, and is holding a baseball cap in his right hand. His dark hair is parted in the middle and slicked back with Vitalis or Brylcreem. He left grease spots wherever he laid his head. My father, twenty-eight, is dressed in a business suit, white shirt, and striped tie. He wears a handkerchief in his breast pocket. His neat, short, dark hair is cut exactly as it is now that it is gray and white.

I don't look like either of these two men. I look like my mother. I'm a little blond three-year-old wearing a double-breasted topcoat over a striped t-shirt and shorts. I am holding a small baseball bat as though it were a cane. The child, as Wordsworth counterintuitively tells us, is father of the man. We become our fathers. Well, almost.

I am a family man. That's a bit unfair, because all three EABs were family men, but somehow being a husband and father defines me more than it did my father or grandfather. They had a work life away from home. I don't. Carolyn and I are equal partners in raising and supporting a family in ways that my grandparents and parents didn't get to be, didn't have to be. Consequently, I have spent a lot more time with my kids than my father and grandfather did with theirs. What defined fathers in the previous two generations was often their absence.

My grandfather was a man's man, a company man, a sportsman, a hunter, a baseball player, a card player, a whiskey drinker. He was the boss at work and the provider at home, the king of his castle. My grandmother never worked outside the home, never learned to drive a car.

My father, for all his affability, is something of a loner, a salesman, a sailor, a merchant marine captain, a veteran of Korea and World War II, a member of the Greatest Generation. In many ways, his has been a life of sacrifice, but he has lived it well, willingly and without complaint. He worked a lot harder for a lot less than his father did, and I just want him to know this Father's Day that I appreciate that. You did a great job, Dad. Thank you.

## AFTER THE PROM

Yarmouth High School's post-prom party was being held in
a field across from the dump out on the edge of town. When
I pulled up at the site shortly before midnight, a handful of
students had already arrived. The first person I saw was one
of my daughters' friends, a varsity athlete, smoking a ciga-
rette. As I got out of my car, a young man I knew by sight
but not by name walked past me holding what looked to be
a can of Budweiser in his hand.

"Hey, Mr. Beem. How's it going?"

As a parent and as a school committee member, my
instinct was to confiscate the beer and remind the young
man that the drinking age in Maine is twenty-one, but this
wasn't my property, my party, or, on this particular night,
my role. I was a self-appointed watchdog, here simply to
make sure that no one who might have been drinking got
behind the wheel of a car. So I just nodded and said nothing.
The fact that the young man made no effort to conceal his
beer made me feel complicit. I didn't want him to think I

condoned underage drinking, but I also didn't want to undermine what little authority the students granted me by hassling them.

The owners of the field knew about the party but were away for the weekend. When I had learned about the party the day before the prom, I had called Neil Shankman, co-chair of the chemical-free Project Graduation committee, and we had decided that the only thing we could do to protect our kids, their friends, and classmates was to attend the party as gatekeepers. Neil arrived minutes after I did and we established a checkpoint in the driveway in front of the house and waited. We didn't have to wait long.

The kids seemed to arrive all at once, and the situation threatened to get out of hand before the prom party even started. The first car to arrive was a stretch limo that was too big to negotiate the drive across the lawn and around the garage to the field. With the limo blocking the driveway, a dozen cars full of kids from the prom backed up in the roadway. Waving flashlights and shouting directions, Neil and I struggled to get the limousine out of the way and to keep cars from parking illegally.

We had stopped by the police station to let the local police know what was going on, and a patrol car arrived on the scene just as the traffic jam was occurring. I ran up and down the side of the road telling kids that they had to park out back in the field but that they'd have to come back in a few minutes after the limo left. The police surveyed the situation, made their presence known, and drove on down the road.

Once we got the limo out of the driveway, carloads of kids began filling up the field behind the house. By 1:00 A.M., there were close to 90 cars and 250 students—roughly half the student body of Yarmouth High School—in the field. Neil and I bundled up in lawn chairs on the driveway and the kids partied all night out back. They built a bonfire in half of an oil tank provided for that purpose, set up tents, turned on tape decks and CD players, listened to Phish, Korn, and the Dave Matthews Band, laughed, and talked about the prom, their impending graduation, and their college plans. And, yes, some drank beer.

Yarmouth High School, like most American high schools, has a zero tolerance policy when it comes to drinking and drugs, but the reality is that the majority of teenagers will try alcohol and marijuana before they graduate. Prohibition didn't work in the 1920s and "Just Say No" doesn't work today. All night long I kept telling myself that as a school committee member I supported the policy, but as a parent I had to deal with the reality.

My daughters, Hannah, then eighteen, and Nora, then sixteen, were out there in that field. They insisted they knew enough not to drink and drive, or to get in a car with someone who had been drinking, but kids are just too vulnerable on prom night. So when I told them that the only way they were going to stay out all night at a party was if I went too, they said okay. In fact, they actually seemed to appreciate what I was trying to do.

I saw Hannah and Nora and their boyfriends when they arrived, but I never saw them again after that. In fact, I only occasionally saw any of the kids after the party got underway. Neil and I hunkered down uncomfortably on the lawn chairs while the kids partied. About every half hour, the same couple, a very bright young man and a very athletic young woman, walked through the dark yard, deep in one of those philosophical discussions only the young can have. They must have walked the perimeter of the property a dozen times during the night.

Shivering beneath a blanket, I remembered being eighteen. I remembered feeling immortal, knowing all the answers, believing that no one had ever felt the things I felt or thought the thoughts I thought, vowing that I would never become as hypocritical as most of the adults I knew. But how do you keep your kids from doing the things you did when you were young?

I graduated from Westbrook (Maine) High School in 1967. When I think of the things we did back then, I know why I felt I had to be at the prom party. Prom nights in the 1960s, we'd pile into a car with a six-pack or two and cruise the back roads around Sebago Lake chasing rumors of parties at someone's camp. I remember one night in particular when I found myself in a carload of upperclassmen going a hundred miles per hour on a narrow, crowned country road. I was scared to death, but I didn't dare say so. Of course we all could have been killed. Sometimes I wonder why we weren't.

Parents in those days seemed largely clueless. They practiced what we now call a "don't ask/don't tell" philosophy. But surely they must have had some idea what their kids were up to; they had done the same things when they were young.

So I kind of envied our kids their big blowout, but, at fifty, I was too old to be pulling an all-nighter. I could feel my mortality in my bones and in the longing for sleep. I wasn't at all sure if what I was doing was right. Somewhere in my thirties, a paradigm shift had occurred. Now I routinely made the mistake of thinking that *everyone* felt the way I felt, thought the way I thought. As uneasy as it made me to be present where teenagers were drinking however, I still recognized the hypocrisy of treating eighteen-year-olds as children. They can vote, go to war, get married, have children, drive cars, own property, but they can't drink.

As Neil and I talked quietly in order to stay awake, I kept thinking about all the things that could go wrong— fights, accidents, date rape, illness, complaints to the police, trespass, damage to the property. Would I be liable if, despite my good intentions and best efforts, something went terribly wrong?

In the wee hours, several other parents showed up to offer us coffee and reinforcement, but we really only needed the coffee. Far from being a drunken orgy or rowdy beer bash, the prom party was a terrific celebration.

When one anxious mother asked if she could go out back to see what was going on, I walked to the back of the garage with her. The yard sloped away through a half-dozen gnarled apple trees to the field where hundreds of young people were silhouetted in the firelight. There was music and laughter and wood smoke in the night air. Just for an instant, I longed to be eighteen again.

I was back in my lawn chair, trying not to fall asleep, when two police cars pulled up at the end of the driveway.

"We've had a complaint about noise," the young patrolman told us.

This surprised me since the nearest neighbor was eighty years old and deaf. Standing in the front yard, you could only here the muffled sound of voices and bongo drums if you listened carefully. It turned out, however, that two or three times during the night, when a celebratory cheer went up from the party, the sound had carried up a ravine to a condo development a half-mile away.

"Tell the kids they'll have to quiet down, or we'll have to break up the party."

When I went out back to ask the kids to cut out the cheers and put away the bongo drums, several students saw me coming and stepped away from the bonfire to greet me. They all had cans or bottles in their hands, but I had now become willfully blind. I assume they were drinking beer, but I intentionally didn't look. As soon as I asked two or three students to spread the word that there had been a noise complaint, the bongos stopped, the CD and tape players dropped a few decibels, and night began to bleach into day.

As the thin gray light of dawn illuminated the field, I walked out back again to survey the scene. It looked like a refugee camp or a mini-Woodstock. Most of the remaining revelers were asleep in their tents and cars. A few hardy souls were sitting around the dying embers of the bonfire talking quietly. And a self-appointed cleanup crew was already picking up cans and bottles. By the time the last kids left in the middle of the morning, the only evidence that a party had taken place were the tire tracks leading into the field.

When I left, I was exhausted but relieved. No violence, no vandalism, no vulgarity, and only one noise complaint. Best of all, no drunk driving. About half the kids stayed all night, but when cars had left, Neil and I had interrogated the drivers to make sure they were fit to drive. In only one case did a student attempt to drive who had obviously been drinking. We got him a designated driver and sent him safely on his way.

• • •

The prom party took place on the night of Friday/Saturday, May 21–22, 1999. First thing Monday morning, I stopped by the school superintendent's office to fill him in on what had transpired just in case he got any complaints, but for two weeks after the party, I heard nothing but thank yous from kids and their parents. Then, on June 8, I got a phone call from a reporter with the local newspaper.

"Mr. Beem, is it true that you had a party on prom night at which you furnished alcohol to minors?"

I took a deep breath and, for what would be the first of a hundred times, explained in great detail exactly what I had done and why I had done it. The next morning, "Board member was 'gatekeeper' at party where teens drank" was front-page news.

It seems that a local minister had heard about the party from his church youth group and, rather than call me to ascertain the facts, had called the local news media. For the next four days, the "gatekeeper controversy" was on the front page of the *Portland Press Herald* and on the six and eleven o'clock news on all four television networks. I received over a hundred calls of support as well as calls from radio talk shows from Maine to Texas. The *Boston Globe* carried the story under the headline "Father puts partying teens' life above law." The ABC news magazine *20/20* even filmed a segment on the prom story. I suppose I could have disconnected the phone, but I didn't have anything to hide and, both as a journalist and as an elected public official, I felt I had a responsibility to answer every question asked.

After four days of phone calls, interviews, camera crews in my yard, and sleepless nights, the "gatekeeper controversy" came to a head at a school committee meeting on the morning of Friday, June 11. As I walked downtown to the meeting, I felt like a condemned man until I saw the banner hanging from the Route One overpass on Main Street, Yarmouth's unofficial community bulletin board. It read "Thank You Edgar and Neil for Caring About Us."

The American Legion log cabin where Yarmouth town council and school committee meetings are held was jammed with local residents, parents, students, and the news media. I read a brief statement explaining what I had done and why and then it was the public's turn. The handful of citizens who came expecting me to be ousted from the school committee instead endured an overwhelming outpouring of local support for what Neil and I had done. The president of the senior class presented Neil Shankman and me with thank-you cards signed by the entire senior class. Parents and students thanked us, praised us, and defended us. Of the twenty-seven people who spoke, only three or four were critical of our actions.

The testimony that meant the most to me came from Doug Carney, the father of one of Nora's field hockey teammates. When Doug stepped to the microphone and prefaced his remarks by saying that at 7:00 A.M. on October 29, 1960, his father had awakened him to tell him that his brother had been killed in an alcohol-related auto accident, my heart sank. I felt sure he would condemn any action that might be construed as condoning teen drinking. I was wrong.

"They had two choices," Doug Carney said. "One was to protect their children and their friends, the other was to uphold the law. I would support their decision 365 days a year, and I thank them."

Throughout the meeting Hannah and two dozen of her senior classmates stood at the back of the room. I had known most of them since they were babies. I had seen some of them baptized, supervised them in nursery school, taught them in Sunday school, taken them on field trips to Boston, coached them on the softball field, and cheered them in plays, field hockey, and soccer games. Now they were about to graduate from high school and take that first big step out into the world. Tears filled my eyes when I tried to explain that I just couldn't stay home on prom night and risk the chance that one night of foolishness might keep any of them from taking that step.

I looked at Hannah, now a young woman about to go off to art school, and I thought of all the decisions my wife Carolyn and I had had to make over the past eighteen years to get her to this point in her young life. When had she been old enough to ride her bike around the block? To walk to school by herself? To stay home alone? To get her ears pierced? To go out on a date? To drive out of town? To be trusted not to get into a car with someone who has been drinking? Where, ultimately, does a responsible parent draw the line?

On June 19, one week after that cathartic school committee meeting, a seventeen-year-old student from Bowdoin, Maine, just twenty miles north of Yarmouth, was killed in a drunk-driving accident following an all-night party. His father was convicted of furnishing a place for minors to drink. Could that have been Hannah? Could that have been me?

At times, I like to think we prevented a similar tragedy by being at the party. Other times, I shudder to think what might have happened despite our good intentions and best efforts. I'm still not sure I did the right thing, but my daughters are.

In the aftermath of the prom party episode, my relationship with my teenaged daughters has, if anything, improved.

"I would never have asked you to do what you did, Dad," Hannah said the other day, "but it didn't surprise me. It just seemed natural for you to be there. Everything you've ever done has been to protect us."

And Nora, who for a long time wouldn't take "No" for an answer to any request, has become far more reasonable when we do find it necessary to draw the line.

"I know you've always said you never say 'No' without a good reason, Dad," Nora said, "but I finally realized that you meant it. You understood how important prom night is to us and you risked your reputation to keep us safe."

Still, I have no idea what she is going to say or what I'm going to do when, come spring, I have to ask once again, "What are you doing after the prom, Nora?"

# FORGIVE ME FOR SAYING SO

A couple of weeks ago, a neighbor up the road called to take issue with my strident opposition to the proposed Taxpayers' Bill of Rights (TABOR). Why she thought she could persuade me that I was wrong and that there was merit in that insidious scheme is beyond me. The conversation ended abruptly when she cited an analysis put out by the Maine Heritage Policy Center, authors of the referendum, and I dismissed MHPC as "a right-wing wacko group."

A few days later, upon reflection, I sent the caller a card, apologizing for the fact that the conversation ended badly and assuring her that I actually get along quite nicely with a lot of people with whom I disagree vehemently on the issues. The list of conservative Republicans whose company I enjoy might surprise you.

I am nothing if not opinionated, outspoken, argumentative, and confrontational. It's always been that way and probably always will be. That's why I need forgiveness—

not because I am necessarily wrong, but because I am often abrasive and sometimes unkind.

"It's not what you say," my mother used to tell me, "it's how you say it."

Every night when I go to bed I pray for forgiveness of the great sins of my past (which we will not go into here or anywhere) and for my sins of the day, which I hope are not too great. I am a pretty shallow and shaky Christian, but I do embrace the concept of forgiveness wholeheartedly— though not, I confess, as wholeheartedly as the Amish. As cranky and ill-tempered as I can be, I like to believe I am also quick to forgive and forget.

When I served on the Yarmouth school committee (1995–2001), one of the guiding principles was to "be hard on issues, not on people." I'm afraid I often violated this rule. Sometimes, in the heat of battle, I am unable to separate the opinion from the person holding it.

My stormy tenure on the school committee began when I was attacked on candidates' night for calling school budget critics "cheapskates" (which I still believe they are, by the way) and for questioning one of my fiscally conservative opponent's commitment to education. I now count this man as a friend.

The controversies carried through to budget hearings, where the biggest critic of school spending was a woman I have come to admire greatly, and to policy debates, where I often found myself at odds with staff members and fellow committee members whom I respect enormously. The storm peaked in 1999 with "The Prom Fiasco," the night another father and I attempted to keep kids safe at a big after-prom party by sitting up all night in the driveway to prevent them from driving drunk. I now get along very well with several people who publicly called for my ouster, and I like to think they forgave me once it became clear to them that I sincerely meant well.

Last week, I had another spirited exchange (of e-mails this time) about TABOR with another woman in town. We grew up in the same town, her dad was the assistant principal at my high school, we served together on the Yarmouth school committee, and our daughters are soccer teammates, so I was particularly upset to find that she supported TABOR, a measure I see as a threat to education funding. When the electronic dust cleared, I got an e-mail from her that asked, "Still friends?"

You bet. Forgiveness, on this mortal plane anyway, is a two-way street. I often seek it and I grant it freely. I subscribe to Blanche Dubois's dictum in Tennessee Williams's *A Streetcar Named Desire*—"Deliberate cruelty is the one unforgivable thing."

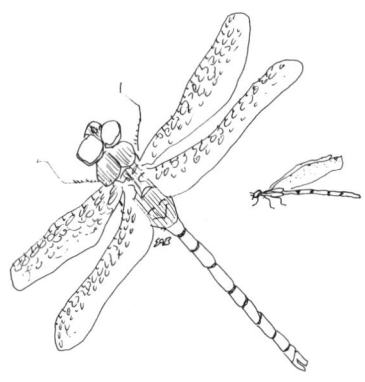

# THE SPIRIT OF THE DRAGONFLY

Just back from our camp at Thompson Lake in Otisfield and I'm happy to report that the dragonflies seem to have hatched in record numbers. The lakeshore and camp roads are alive with swooping, darting, hovering, and patrolling odonata, among the most elegant and engaging of God's creatures with whom we share this Earth.

If I were to get a tattoo (and the chances of that seem fairly remote), I would get a dragonfly tattooed on my left shoulder. Specifically, I would get the likeness of the common green darner (*Anax junius*), that handsome entomological copter with the big green eyes and iridescent blue thorax. So common, yet so exotic in flight and form and color.

Dragonflies are charismatic microfauna. They are among the very few insects most people don't mind landing on them. Not only do they mean us no harm, they eat enormous amounts of mosquitoes and black flies, and best of all, they sometimes even seem curious about us, something we humans find hard to resist. Not only will dragonflies cruising the lake stop to rest on an oar or paddle, they often land on the paddler as well. I have even stood still with outstretched hand and invited dragonflies and damselflies to light. You can tell when they're checking you out, because they come closer with each pass.

It's a wonder dragonflies have time for us, however, their lives being so brief, perhaps five to ten weeks. Having spent most of their lives as underwater nymphs, they emerge when the water heats up, climb out into the sun, and shed their larval shells, leaving behind transparent little dinosaurs on the rocks and docks along the shore. Then they flutter off as tenerals into the bushes until they have dried and hardened.

When last I checked, 158 of the 435 known species of dragonflies and damselflies occur in Maine. Dragonflies are larger than damselflies, have eyes that meet at the top, and perch with their four gossamer wings spread. Damselflies are more delicate, have eyes that are separated, and perch with their wings raised above their backs.

A couple of summers back, while researching an article on the "Maine Damselfly and Dragonfly Survey" (http://mdds.umf.maine.edu/~odonata), I had the pleasure of taking my daughter Tess, then ten, with me to watch Inland Fish & Wildlife biologist Phillip deMaynardier track the elusive New England bluet around a boggy pond in Sanford. It wasn't long before Tess was knee-deep in muck, netting and identifying sedge sprites, ebony jewel wings, common whitetail skimmers, and eastern forktails. With a swipe of the net and a flick of the wrist, she'd intercept their flight then gently remove them, holding their wings delicately between middle and index finger. Phillip examined each catch, pointing out the identifying markings and the unique shapes of their male termini, or claspers.

Dragonflies are aerial lovers. The male tows the female through the air, having clasped her behind the head with claspers that are unique to each species. The female then bends her thorax to the male's so that the mating pair forms a flying wheel. Once fertilized, the female then deposits her eggs underwater to start the cycle of life again.

These winged beings, their huge eyes containing as many as 30,000 receptors, whiz about the world at speeds up to thirty-five mph, taking in everything that moves. I'm still not sure why I am so attracted to them, but I do tend to regard dragonflies as personal totem animals. Perhaps it's just that dragonflies, haunters of the bogs, cruisers of the rivers and streams, patrollers of the lakes, seem to embody the spirit of Maine. Sprightly avatars of Maine summer, their lives, like the season, are so very brief and so very beautiful.

## FUN AND FUNDS
## AT THE CLAM FESTIVAL

The thing that still surprises me after all these years in town is that the Yarmouth Clam Festival is in Yarmouth at all. I mean a Scarborough Clam Festival would make more sense, right? Yarmouth isn't a big clam-digging town, after all. Come to think of it, the 5,000 gallons of clams that will be consumed at the festival come from Canada—a good thing now that red tide has closed most of the Maine coast to clamming.

What a lot of people don't get about the Clam Festival is that it's not really about clams at all. It started out some forty-odd years ago as a kind of firemen's muster, old-home-days town picnic. It's still about food and fun of course, but, at its heart, the Clam Festival is now a spectacularly successful community fundraiser.

Almost every church, civic, and boosters group in town makes a ton of money during Clam Festival. It's a good time and good food for good causes. So please, all you big-time bike racers, don't have a hissy fit first thing Sunday morning when the soccer boosters ask you to pay to park out behind town hall. Sure, we want you to have fun, but the festival isn't about you, it's about fundraising.

Virtually every civic-minded citizen of Yarmouth volunteers for one or more organizations during Clam Festival. My own work schedule involves helping to sort and move (if my back allows it) thousands of books for the First Parish Church book sale, cooking hamburgers for the sophomore class, frying hot dogs for the church during Friday's kickoff parade, organizing the early morning cleanup crew that rakes the Village Green and the North Yarmouth Academy lawn Saturday and Sunday mornings on behalf of the Yarmouth Lacrosse Boosters, taking a shift or two at the Yarmouth Soccer Boosters parking lot, and helping with the cleanup at the church Sunday afternoon when the festival is over.

That may sound like a lot, but it's really not. There are a lot of folks who spend the entire weekend working at the Clam Festival and a few, like Mike Lutz who heads up Clam Festival activities for our church, who spend weeks preparing for, coordinating, and cleaning up after the Clam Festival.

Festival as a noisy, congested nuisance, but once the kids got into school I finally realized that the best way to enjoy the Yarmouth Clam Festival is to work at it. With 120,000 fun-seekers invading town over the weekend, it's more fun to be behind the scenes than it is to be milling around aimlessly with the throng. The people-watching is great, you see folks you haven't seen all year, and pumping out hundreds of hot dogs an hour gives you a sense of purpose and satisfaction that is hard to beat.

Professionals who study the science of happiness have found that the happiest people on Earth are those who are surrounded by a supportive network of family and friends. That being so, the Yarmouth Clam Festival is one of the greatest sources of happiness here in Yarmouth. Everyone pitching in for a good cause creates a sense of fellowship that lasts long after the grease stains left on the baseball field by Smokey's Greater Shows are gone. And the fact that close to a million dollars changes hands over the weekend doesn't hurt our public spirit either.

# TRACKING SUBURBAN WILDLIFE

Forget foreign policy, growth management, environmental preservation, property taxes, and school funding. The major issue at the moment on our quarter-acre is the groundhog who has burrowed in beneath the brush pile in the back yard. Carolyn is worried about her tender basil and I'm in a moral dilemma over whether and, if so, how to get rid of the critter. One of my neighbors dispatched a groundhog in his woodpile a couple of years back with a pistol, but the memory of the repeated *crack* of gunshots in our quiet neighborhood still makes me shudder, and anyway, I don't own a gun —unless you count the pellet gun I was given last summer to arm myself against an onslaught of red squirrels.

I suppose I could track down a Havahart trap and simply move the woodchuck out of town, but I'm not sure I really want to do that. As long as he doesn't devastate the garden (which is only fifteen feet away from the brush pile), I kind of like the idea of sharing the property with another significant mammal. Don't get me wrong; I'm not a hunter, but I'm not an animal rights activist either. I just enjoy the surprising variety of wildlife to be found in our little patch of suburbia.

Our yard backs up to railroad tracks and is bounded on two sides by vestigial woods. Deer frequently browse along the tracks and, in the evening, a family of coyotes yips and howls in the woods and fields beyond the tracks. Almost nightly, one creature or another appears from the woods to explore the yard and test our goodwill.

In a lot of ways, the animals around here might be considered pests, but I'm more than willing to put up with a little stolen birdseed, a few lost stems of basil, and the occasional trash can raid in return for the pleasure of watching other species go about the earnest business of survival. To date, we haven't suffered any real damage, though I suspect those unseen coyotes may have been complicit in the disappearance of one of our cats, herself an ancient, inveterate night-stalker.

It's possible that, should I ever tear off the roof boards, I will find that the hibernal scratching under our eaves will turn out to be a family of red squirrels who very well may have done some internal damage, but I have more or less made peace with these irritable intruders. For a few summers, I tried driving the red squirrels away from our bird feeders with a well-aimed garden hose, but I started feeling like a bully after I soaked a couple of them pretty good on a rather chilly summer evening. Now I just approach them slowly, they protest, throw a little chattering fit, bluff a charge, then dash off angrily, only to return as soon as the coast is clear.

I make it a point not to tangle with the gorgeous big

skunk that patrols the side yard around midnight and even ventures up onto the back porch if I am lazy enough to leave a trash bag out there overnight. The same goes for the rare raccoon that gets surprised and treed in the spruce from which the bird feeder hangs. The last one I saw looked like a small bear and made some most unpleasant noises when I snapped on the back-porch light and stepped out for some air.

These big critters are far outnumbered, however, by the gangs of gray squirrels who pass through the yard and the sacrificial ranks of moles, voles, and field mice that turn up disemboweled and headless on the back steps after a night of kitty hunting. But the predominant wild presence here-abouts is the nocturnal chorus of croaks and trills coming from the shallow swamp pond just through the trees where, I suspect, an amphibian orgy takes place nightly. Later in the summer, little gem-like tree frogs start appearing on the ferns at the back door and suctioned onto the bathroom window. Fine, delicate, colorful little beings, those tree frogs. Who wouldn't want them around the house?

The groundhog, however, is another story. I'm pretty sure Carolyn is going to want him evicted. Which seems kind of a shame. For one thing, I'm really not up to the job. For another, the life of the groundhog strikes me as quite instructive. They mind their own business, love the sun, and duck for cover at the slightest threat, something we higher animals are having to re-learn in this new age of anxiety.

# REMEMBER THE BEACH

There were summers past when we managed to spend almost every sunny day at the beach, but this year July has flown and we have not been once. Not sure what to make of this. Getting old, I guess. Still, it doesn't seem like summer unless we get to the beach.

Back in high school, I used to put a buddy on the back of the All-State scooter and motor out to Higgins Beach, buy a pack of Parliaments at the beach store, and lie on the sand all day smoking and watching girls. Then parking became impossible at Higgins, seaweed washed up on the beach, and our youth moved on to Scarborough Beach.

The summer before we were married, we went to Scarborough Beach all the time. We'd walk way down to the left beyond the limits of the lifeguards so we could be alone and in love. Scarborough Beach has those clear class distinctions—rich summer folks at the Prouts Neck end, the public in the middle, the wealthy patrons (now condo dwellers) of the Atlantic House at the other end. Between the state park

and the largely unused Atlantic House beach, there are a few
hundred yards of no man's sand, perfect for beachcombers,
surfers, surfcasters, and lovers.

Remember when the sun wouldn't kill you? In those
Higgins Beach days, we'd slather on baby oil and broil all
day, get as brown as possible as fast as possible. Forty years
on, we carry reminders of those hot, careless days in the
form of wrinkles, blotches, and spots, a small price to pay for
such pleasures, unless, of course, they turn cancerous.

This being cold, damp Maine, we still have a strong,
primordial urge to return to the sea and bake in the sun.
These days, of course, we are more careful, covering every
inch of exposed skin with sunscreen, wearing t-shirts to
cover our soft, mottled bodies and baseball caps to keep the
sun out of our eyes.

Even when the girls were little, we have always taken a
minimalist approach to beach-going. The beach bag in the
bathroom closet is always ready to go and has everything we
need—bathing suits, towels, beach blanket, sunscreen, t-
shirts. That's about it. Grab a thermos of lemonade and a
few pieces of fruit and go. No books, no toys, no music, no
chairs. And certainly, no umbrellas. When we see families
arriving at the beach towing surfboards, wetsuits, boogie
boards, Frisbees, footballs, inner tubes, beach chairs, umbrellas, coolers, even pop-up tents, we feel kind of sorry for
them. The beach is such a gloriously elemental place. There's
no need for such frills.

Here's what you do. You drop your blanket and bag on a
vacant patch of sand and walk down to the water. If you're
young and fit and immortal, plunge right in. If you're old
and wise and afraid of heart attacks, splash a little of the cold

North Atlantic on your face, your arms, your belly, your back. Ease in. Enjoy the astringent, salty chill. Inhale involuntarily when the brine hits your groin. Stand in the ocean up to your hips and wait for the next sizable wave. As the wave approaches, launch yourself up and out to match its arc and angle. A few kicks and the sea should propel you toward shore, shooting you forward in a roil of foam. If you have done so correctly, the wave should deposit you on the sand, washed up and happy.

Do this repeatedly until you are numb with cold, until your ears ache, until you have vertigo. Then stagger back to your blanket, lie down on a towel, and bake the life back into your bones. The sun won't kill you. At least not today.

Later, there will be tide pools to explore at the far end of the beach, crabs scuttering beneath the rockweed, snails and periwinkles aplenty, even the occasional urchin. And there will surely be treasures to be found along the hot sands— tiny jewels of sea glass, rings of lobster claw elastics, and bracelets of brightly colored plastic trap markers; perhaps, if you're lucky, a particolored foam buoy and a length of useful braided line, a sand dollar negotiable in a better world, a littoral world.

Stay until the sun is too far inland to matter any more, until the fair-weather beach-goers and overburdened families are gone, until the lifeguards have completed their day's-end swim alongshore, until Tom the parking lot attendant has gone home for the night. Sleep if you must. There is no better sleep than a nap on the beach.

On the way home, stop for Needham ice cream cones. And when you get home, don't be in too much of a hurry to shower. The sand and salt crunchy on your skin is good for you, natural, a reminder that you are, after all, an animal. And when you do shower you wash away the summer, not just the sand and salt but the tan and burn as well. Standing in the porcelain tub, as white as a perch, as pale as a corpse, remember the beach. It won't be summer much longer. It will be winter soon enough.

# THE WAY TO PICK BERRIES

The way to pick berries is on your knees, a supplicant to ripe nature, the blood of the fruit staining your knees. If you take the arrogant two-legged human stance for too long, you're apt to become distracted by the promise of more and bigger and brighter in the next row, the next patch. Better to settle in, take the more humble view of deer, bear, fox, raccoon, and pluck the hidden, hanging jewels close at hand in the cool, leafy understory of the bramble.

Raspberries are such delicate fruit, so complex in structure yet so easily damaged. The hollowed geometry of their drupelets does not bear the weight of a quart box willingly. Their measure is the pint, the half-pint. Taking more at a time than will fit reverentially in two cupped hands is excess.

In an afternoon breeze, raspberries will also elude you, tantalize you with a brazen flash of their pinkness only to duck modestly behind the green skirt of a leaf or the prickly protection of a cane. They want to be enticed from the core rather than grabbed or pulled. This insistence on gentleness may have something to do with the fact that, despite their name, raspberries are not berries at all, but rather a sweet, aggregate fruit of the rose family.

Now you may stoop to pick strawberries if you must, but the best way is still on hands and knees, pushing the waxy box along through the straw and trampled berries. The best berries grow beneath the bowed stems and leaves, which must be lifted like the hem of a dress to reveal the treasures beneath, ovate clusters ranging in color by ripeness from blood clot crimson to strawberry blond.

There is an anxiety about picking strawberries that is one part competition and two parts scale. Picking a quart is nothing; picking a fifteen-pound flat can be worrisome, the berries being so small in proportion to the container. It seems to take forever to cover the bottom. Other pickers may stray into your row, straddle rows, cut in up ahead, lured out of line by the abundance by rights assigned to you by the Jamaican field hand. Relax. There are plenty of berries for everyone—the old grannies, the young lovers, the suburban mothers herding youngsters who eat as much as they pick.

Blueberries are another story altogether. Certainly, you may rake your way through the barrens, feet splayed, back bent and aching, long tines ripping through the bushes, pail filling with the tiny round berries with jaunty, flared crowns. The litter of leaves can be winnowed later. To rake a bucket of wild blueberries is to hold a Maine summer in your hands, a harvest as valuable in the toil as in the mouth. To pick them one at a time by hand is a test of patience and perseverance beyond most of us. Hats off to the mothers and the bears who do.

And what of blackberries, the sweetest and seediest of all

Maine berries? Find a cellar hole, find a blackberry patch. Or so it was when we were young. But now there are camps and condos and mini-malls where abandoned farms and vacant lots and overgrown tote roads once invited blackberries.

So find a farmer, drive up her dusty driveway, and pick your blackberries a quart at a time off her porch. Lift the little tent of netting that keeps the bees off. Remove a box or two. Replace the tent. Place your money in the coffee can or the mason jar. Pay whatever she asks and be grateful. The blackberries, so rare, a mouthful of juice and wood and history, will soon be gone. Count your blessings.

## THE FRUITS OF SUMMER

Carolyn and I had only been married a short time when I discovered that she is part bear—at least when it comes to berrying. Set her down in a blueberry barren or blackberry patch and she's in her natural element. When the two older girls were just cubs, she would haul them off down a power line somewhere and pick blueberries by hand, no rake, just *ka-plink, ka-plank, ka-plunk* as in Robert McCloskey's classic tale of summer innocence, *Blueberries for Sal.*

In recent years, we've been raking our berries up on Allen Hill at Henrickson's U-Rake Blueberries in Oxford. A tractor-drawn wagon takes you up to the forty-acre barrens, where you're issued a rake and a bucket and I can tell it bothers Carolyn that it only takes us ten or fifteen minutes to rake more berries than we could pick by hand in an hour or two. Back down in the barnyard, the leaves and twigs are blown from our berries by a 150-year-old winnowing machine and we're ready to hit the road all too soon. In fact, when Henrickson's didn't have enough berries on hand to sell to a customer who couldn't rake his own, Carolyn let them sell some of hers and even offered to go back and rake more.

Not only does she love gathering berries, she is also thrifty by nature and gets obvious pleasure from the fact that she's only paying seventy-five cents a pound. In truth, she'd probably pay Henrickson's to let her rake.

So we already had sixteen pounds of fresh frozen blueberries in our fridge last week when we took a little vacation trip up to Mount Desert Island. On the way back down, however, Carolyn couldn't resist a "Wild Maine Blueberries" sign on the side of Route One and ended up purchasing another five pounds. Then the very next day, dispatched to Cherryfield on L.L. Bean business, Carolyn came home with another seven quarts.

Since the freezer compartment is already full of blueberries and the strawberries we picked at Maxwell's in Cape Elizabeth and Gillespie's in New Gloucester, we're eating blueberries as fast as we can. Carolyn tells me that recent research has suggested that blueberries improve memory, but the fact that I just had to go out in the back yard to ask her what she had told me blueberries were good for casts some doubt on those findings.

Carolyn is out in the garden at the moment picking Japanese beetles off her raspberry plants, something she does religiously every evening when she gets home from work. In truth, we've had mixed results with raspberries. We'll get a good crop one year and then either cut them back when we shouldn't or not cut them back when we should—I can't remember which it is. So, for raspberries, we are largely dependent on the kindness of a neighbor with a thriving raspberry patch—a neighbor Carolyn softens up with quarts of our excess blueberries.

A few years back, we suffered what I have come to think of as the Great Berry Disaster of '94 when the chest freezer in the basement died and we didn't realize it until the smell of fermenting berries started to permeate the house. Carolyn has never fully recovered from losing two season's worth of frozen berries, so we have never replaced the old chest freezer, preferring to have our cache of berries right in the kitchen where she can keep an eye on it.

The task at hand at the moment is trying to find an alternative source of blackberries. Our primary source is a farm up on Mayberry Hill in Casco, but you have to be passing by when the little "Blackberries" sign is out at the end of the driveway. At any given time, the blackberry lady only has four to six quarts set out for sale on her porch and somehow that's never enough.

There used to be blackberry patches all around our camp at Thompson Lake in Otisfield, but over the past fifteen to twenty years most of the patches have disappeared, the victims of development as suburbia creeps inexorably out into the countryside. Sooo—should any generous-spirited berry-picker happen to know of a good source of those blue-black jewels of summer, I can assure you that Carolyn can be very discreet when it comes to the location of wild berries.

## EMPTY NEST

The dog died in May. Now the bird is gone. Not dead.
Gone. Escaped. Flew the coop.

Most of the time I tended to forget that we had a parakeet. It didn't even have a name other than Birdie. I was
reminded of its existence within our household every once in
awhile, though, when conducting telephone interviews. In
the middle of a conversation, the person on the other end of
the line would interrupt to ask, "Do you have a bird?"

"A parakeet. Why?"

"I can hear it chirping in the background."

I had become so used to Birdie's chirps that I no longer
heard them except when he was out of birdseed and elevated
them to an ear-splitting screech. This morning I got up at six
and spent an hour in the back yard listening for that chirp,
that screech. If I heard it amidst the chatter of the wild birds,
I didn't recognize it.

Carolyn had taken the cage outside the evening before to
clean it. She often took the bird outside in the summer so it

could talk to the other birds. This time, however, Birdie made a break for it, slipping out the half-opened door and flapping unceremoniously to a branch some twenty feet up a tree in the yard. Carolyn and I spent the evening swatting mosquitoes and trying to coax the parakeet down from its perch. I even tried raising a long branch up to it, but each time I did it just flew to a higher branch.

Being a person of the book, the first thing I did when Birdie got loose was to dig out the parakeet guide to see if it said anything about what to do when they escape. Not a word.

Climbing the tree was out of the question. Trying to squirt him down with the garden hose didn't seem like such a great idea. So we decided to leave his green metal cage open with food in it, figuring he always returned to his cage when he flew around in the house. It didn't work.

Perhaps Birdie just heard the call of the wild. She may be in the woods behind the house, but if so I cannot discern her captive call from that of the free birds. It'll give me something to do for the next week or so as I work around the yard, but I have no real hope of ever getting her back.

I suppose we all suffer from the illusion of control, so we naturally feel helpless when we realize that we cannot control everything in our lives. For the past few decades, my life has been about bringing up three daughters. Now two of those girls are young women, out on their own, fledged, flown the coop, empty nest. And the baby, now a senior, tried her own wings out two summers back, spending five weeks away from home, first on a two-week trip to Europe, then on a two-week soccer trip to England and Scotland followed by a week at the beach with friends.

Freedom is fraught with dangers. It makes me anxious to have my girls out in the world where I can no longer protect them—if I ever really could. I'm having trouble letting go. I liked it better when the house was full of kids—and dogs and birds. All of a sudden, it's getting way too quiet around here.

## SAVING THE BIRD TREE

For the past ten years or so, Carolyn has been begging me to chop down the big Norway spruce growing outside the kitchen window. Twenty-five years ago, when we moved in, the spruce was small enough that I could almost see over it. Over the course of the next couple of decades, however, it grew up and out such that its prickly skirt (not to mention its roots) almost touched the foundation. So a few years ago I limbed the tree up to a height of six feet so we could walk around and under it. That little bit of tree surgery will ultimately, I fear, spell its demise.

Now Carolyn wants a deck built on the back of the house and the big, spindly spruce is smack in the way. It is now thirty feet tall, only the top six feet or so of which are still green. The rest of the tree consists of dead and dying branches and that knobby, pitch-oozing trunk. My effort to spare it seems to have turned something beautiful into something ugly.

My attachment to that old gray ghost of tree, however,

has nothing to do with its appearance and everything to do with its function. I call it the bird tree, because the cylindrical feeder full of black oil sunflower seeds attracts birds from dawn till dusk. The chickadees think they own it, but they reluctantly share the bird tree daily with the nuthatch and the titmouse, the juncos and goldfinches, the cardinals and jays, redwing blackbirds from the nearby swamp, and the endless procession of gray and red squirrels and the occasional chipmunk. Come nightfall, the bird tree attracts a family of raccoons from the woods out back as well as an occasional visit from a rare flying squirrel. As often as not, we find the feeder ransacked and empty on the ground at daybreak.

My love of the bird tree, of course, is selfish. My sunroom office looks out on the back yard and the seedy, winged society the tree encourages is my work environment. While Tess goes off to school each day with hundreds of high school classmates and Carolyn goes off to work with thousands of fellow L.L. Bean employees, I am left home alone with the birds to keep me company.

Carolyn argues that it is the bird feeder, not the tree, that attracts the birds, but there is no other tree suitable for a feeder close to the house. We will plant a peach, pear, or plum tree, she promises, but I worry that some fruiting nursery sapling will not provide the ample shelter, shade, and perches that the bird tree affords, at least not in my lifetime.

I'm sure that my lovely wife, who talks to plants as much as I talk to birds, counts my resistance to chopping down the bird tree as yet another instance of my fear of change, and she may be right. Change may be the only constant, but I have concluded that very few changes are for the better. I may be able to hold out a bit longer, weeks, perhaps months, but I have the feeling the bird tree's days are numbered.

# HOME ALONE

For a brief period twenty-four years ago I lived alone and actually enjoyed it. Or, at least, I seem to recall that I did. It was only for six or eight months and it was also the only time in my life that I was not living with someone—parents, roommate, wife, and children. Actually, it may only have been the first few heady days of independence that I enjoyed. I remember coming home from work at the Portland Public Library one evening and realizing that no one on Earth knew where I was, what I was doing, or even cared. No expectations. No demands on my time. Total freedom. I could do anything I wanted. I promptly arranged to get married.

As I write this, I have been home alone now for nine days, less than halfway through the three weeks that Carolyn and the girls are in Europe spending Carolyn's L.L. Bean bonus on a London-Paris-Geneva-Milan juggernaut. I'm getting used to the solitude here on the home front, but I can't actually say that I enjoy it.

When someone asks the inevitable question—"Why didn't you go with them?"—my stock response has been "Because someone had to stay home with the dog." Ritz is elderly and infirm and I doubt he would survive three weeks in a kennel, but that's not the real reason I stayed home. Truth be told, I want Carolyn and the girls to enjoy themselves, and there is a much greater chance of that if I am not along as excess baggage. And, believe me, I come with a lot of baggage—fearful flyer, lousy traveler, control freak, lack spontaneity, need plan, overly critical, complain too much, low energy, need daily nap, creature of habit, etc., etc., etc. Pretty attractive package, hunh?

"So what are you doing with yourself?" folks ask.

"I'm doing what I do best—nothing," I reply.

That's not true either. For those who (like my family) need a serious answer to be satisfied, I say I'm working on a novel, taking three weeks to make a flying start on a book I have been writing since 1976. Actually, I just *plan* to write it; I never actually write it. Well, again not entirely true. The story exists in three different manuscripts and a screenplay—failures all. I have a revision plan in place. It's gonna be great this time, sure to be a book club hit, make a lot of money, etc., etc. It's just that I'm too busy doing nothing to actually write it.

(In the midst of pecking out this column, an e-mail just arrived from Paris, where it sounds as though the cats of Montmartre were the main attraction. "Hope writing is keeping you busy and that you're making lots of money," Daughter No. 2 writes, "'cause we're spending it as fast as humanly possible.")

Actually, girls, I'm not really writing, I'm just puttering.

I've been spending the mornings working on magazine assignments to just keep a little money coming in, but my real focus has been a list of little projects—paint back steps, replace door sill, clean refrigerator out, throw out all sorts of things that no one is going to miss, weed and water garden, pick strawberries, mow lawn, paint dining room. Won't you be surprised when you come home to find the rose pink dining room painted "Afternoon Yellow"?

After making my afternoon rounds—post office, library, supermarket, nap—I've been spending the evenings in a nice little routine I've managed to develop—shoot a few hoops at the middle school parking lot just to move the old bones around, walk the old dog, fix a little supper, watch the Sox lose to whoever they happen to be playing, read until I fall asleep.

Being home alone took a little getting used to. The first week was the hardest. A few frissons of panic when I realized I really was *alone*. But now it's working out quite nicely for me. I just fill the empty hours with busywork and call it a day. As L. Rust Hills wrote in his invaluable Fussy Man guide, *How to Retire at 41,* "You want the feeling of doing something all the time, of being busy and efficient, but you don't want to get too much done. It is an aspect of the working world, this emphasis on *getting things done.* In the no-work world, the idea is not necessarily to get things done, but to *have things to do.*"

The way I look at it, this frittering away my days should be good practice for retirement. In fact, I may already be retired and not know it. I won't know for sure, of course, until Carolyn and the girls get home.

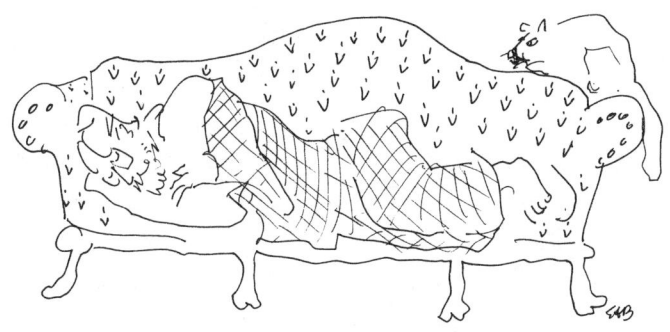

# THE VIRTUE OF LYING

Lying is the most natural thing in the world. We all do it all the time and, if I do say so myself, I am pretty darn good at it. With very little provocation, I'll lie just about anywhere anytime. I think I get it from my father.

Dad is one of the world's great liers. No, not liars; liers. I'm not talking here about prevarication; I'm talking about recumbency. I was lying on a folding cot on the deck of our camp at the lake reading, curiously enough, an essay entitled "Against Exercise," when the utter pleasure of lying still came to me like a static revelation. I sat up and looked down toward the lake where daughter Tess and a friend were lying in the sun on the neighbor's dock, warm and motion- less. A few minutes later when I looked again, they were lying on air mattresses, floating silently, cool and gently rocking, on the surface of the water. So peaceful. So comfort- able. So beautiful.

Lying is a state of pure being. Standing and sitting are evolutionary adaptations to the unnatural verticality of homo sapiens, and running is a social construct, unseemly in all but the young. My generation got just about everything wrong and the terrible battle it wages against gravity and age is one of them. At least that was my reading of Mark Greif's excellent essay (originally published in *n +1* magazine in 2004 and reprinted in *The Best Essays of 2005,* a copy of which I keep at the camp for idle moments), in which young Mr. Greif seems to argue that regimented exercise is something that shouldn't be done in public, gyms being little more than extensions of public toilets.

Lying, on the other hand, whether in public or private, strikes me as completely socially acceptable. The purity of the reclining figure is universal. Even vagrants passed out on park benches have their proper place in the society of the supine.

We all enter this world as babes in bassinets, cradles, and cribs, and most of us leave it lying in coffins or on pyres. In between, we struggle to our feet, make our restive, unsteady ways in the world, and then collapse. Perhaps that's why we love our beds so. We are practicing the ultimate surrender, crawling between the cool sheets and letting go of consciousness, at least for a few hours.

Of course, lying does not necessarily connote sleep. Personally, I do tend to drift off anytime I get more than few degrees below vertical, but lying down can also be relaxing and restorative when you are awake, or so I hear. Lying can be an effective position for reading, watching television, listening to music, sunbathing, gazing at the stars, or even for making love, I suppose, though I don't recommend it. The highest form of lying, however, is lying for its own sake.

There are forms of lying that don't really qualify as lying

at all. Lying down on the couch qualifies, for example, but tipping back in a recliner or in the front seat of your car does not. Hammocks are also vastly overrated as a form of recumbent recreation. Sure, you get rocked gently into unconsciousness, but you're not really lying down, you're just suspended, more like a fish caught in a net than a higher being who has escaped the burden of being erect.

My favorite place to lie is on the beach. I am not sunbathing, mind you, as these days I am generally covered in t-shirts, towels, and lotions after a naked youth of broiling in cocoa butter and baby oil. What I am doing when I am lying on the beach is just being there, listening to the sea and the wind and the birds, smelling the salt and the sunscreen, watching the parade of seaside flesh, feeling the impression my own body makes on the shifting sands.

I am never so alive to the beauty and the majesty and mystery of life on Earth than I am when I am lying on the beach. My salty blood becomes one with the sea, my old bones converse with the mineral bed beneath me. I'd be lying if I said it isn't a religious experience. It is. I just wish I didn't always wake up drooling.

# A WORLD OF MAKE-BELIEVE

On a lovely summer evening last week I was sitting on
the steps watching the world go by when the rows of
hostas growing either side of our front walkway suddenly
reminded me of my childhood. When I was about ten we
lived in a little house that had thick hostas growing along
the driveway. My brother and I and some of the other neighborhood boys played cars and trucks in the driveway, the
hostas becoming trees in the miniature landscape of toy cars
and make-believe.

Back then, I used to think that someday I would own a
real home and a real car, and I wondered whether I would
even remember playing in the driveway, lost in the world of
my imagination. The car I used to push around under the
hostas was a plastic Lincoln Continental and I imagined
myself in the distant future piloting one of those big boats
with its leather interior and cool continental-kit spare tire
mounted on the back. I have never owned a Lincoln Continental, yet it remains my paradigm of automotive coolness.

A lot of our make-believe back in the 1950s involved guns—toy guns, of course, and the fact that I have never wanted to own a real gun suggests to me that playing with guns does not necessarily do irreparable harm to a kid. Under the influence of TV detective shows such as *Peter Gunn, Richard Diamond, Private Detective,* and *77 Sunset Strip,* we would sit in my mother's blue and white '52 Plymouth and pretend to be private eyes on stakeouts.

When not playing detectives, we played cowboys, prepubescent gunslingers inspired by the westerns that dominated the television of the 1950s: *Have Gun, Will Travel, Rawhide, The Rifleman, Wagon Train, Sheriff of Cochise, The Lone Ranger, Gunsmoke, Tombstone Territory, The Nine Lives of Elfego Baca.* What both gumshoes and gunslingers had in common was a sense of tough-guy independence, that kind of Clint Eastwood lone-wolf hero willing to do whatever needed to be done to defeat the bad guys and the forces of evil.

The youthful fantasies that persisted into adolescence tended to concern sports. We knew not only the statistics but also the batting stances and windups of all the Major League players (there were only eight teams in each league back then), and would play entire games imitating the line-ups of the Red Sox, Yankees, Orioles, and Indians. As Jackie Jensen, Jimmy Piersall, and Frank Malzone, I have hit against the likes of Bob Turley, Whitey Ford, and Herb Score.

I stopped consciously making-believe abruptly and embarrassingly in 1962 when, at age thirteen, I was in the midst of a regressive gunfight in the field at the end of our street, savoring the sweet melodrama of getting shot off the top of a pile of loam, just as my eighth-grade girlfriend appeared on the scene. How was I ever going to get her to make out with me again after she had seen me playing cowboys?!

In our teenage years, our make-believe becomes inextricably bound up in our self-image and the identity we imagine for ourselves—ladies' man, athlete, rebel, hood, scholar, clown, whatever it may be. As adults, we tend to think we no longer make believe at all, but I have come to believe that our pretending just becomes more subtle and subverted. Our lives are really just the stories we're telling each other and ourselves. We all have an interior narrative running in the background of our consciousness having to do with who we think we are and what we think the world is all about.

Most of the time, as mature adults, we don't let on (even if we are aware of it) that we are not necessarily the people others think we are. Only when we drop our earnest facades and revert to the playfulness of youth do we reveal something of the story we are telling ourselves. This is nowhere more apparent to me than when I see friends and neighbors dancing. My view of a fair number of all-American soccer moms has changed dramatically after seeing them boogie on the dance floor. They may be pretending to be career women, pillars of the community, polite, prim, and proper, but animated by a good backbeat their bodies tell another story about who they think they are.

Ultimately, this idea that we all have a suppressed narrative about who we are is how I have come to understand the deep divide between staunch Bush supporters and inveterate Bush bashers like myself. (Bet you didn't see that coming.) It's not so much a difference of political philosophy as a difference in the way we imagine ourselves in the world.

I'm tempted to suggest that George W. Bush and his supporters just never got out of the gunslinger fantasy phase, but that's overly simplistic. It's more like the mistakes and failures that were so obvious to those of us who opposed the Bush administration just don't fit the narrative of patriotism, democracy, capitalism, and Christianity that Bush supporters told themselves. Therefore, they couldn't recognize or accept them. Dissent looked unpatriotic to them, whereas those of us who are making believe that peace and justice can be accomplished without violence see dissent as the essence of patriotism. Naturally, I believe that's a better story to be telling oneself.

# THE TRUTH ABOUT
# UNDERWEAR AND SOCKS

In "The Love Song of J. Alfred Prufrock," one of T. S.
Eliot's many melancholy meditations on the passage of time,
the poet wrote, "I have measured out my life in coffee
spoons." Personally, I measure out my life in underwear and
socks. Underwear are my days; socks the seasons of my life.

At last count, I owned nine pairs of cotton boxer shorts,
not including the Union Jack souvenir drawers the girls
brought me from England a few summers back. Four are
staid though colorful plaids, one is a nondescript overall
print, and the other four feature bumblebees, grasshoppers,
alligators, and baby chicks. I mostly wear the plaid these
days, as I am a serious man. I can't quite bring myself to gird
my loins in the British flag, so the Union Jack shorts remain
still-packaged in the back of the underwear and sock drawer.

Being a late bloomer, I was at least thirty years old before
I switched from the white cotton briefs (tightie whities) of
my youth to the more mature (and airier) boxers preferred

by serious men. It's a wonder, in fact, that I had any love life at all before thirty. What woman could possibly get excited about a man in boys' undies?

Now that I am a serious man, I naturally do most of the family laundry. Lately, the passage of time as measured by clean boxers has begun to trouble me. I stand down there in the basement, folding the laundry from the dryer, and I am struck time and time again by the fact that each pair of underwear represents another day passed.

How could there be five pairs of boxers in the wash? Where has the time gone? Almost a week of my life gone in the blink of a rinse cycle. If this memento mori of undergarments continues much longer, I may have to stop wearing underwear altogether. And then how could I possibly consider myself a serious man?

The sock matter is somewhat less pressing but equally as serious. I don't wear socks at all during the summer, so this time of year, when I am forced to inventory my sock drawer against the advancing chill, I am made aware that another season has passed. Soon I will be forced once again to slip back into socks, though I may be able to preserve the illusion of summer a month or so by wearing socks under sandals. Nothing says, "I am a serious man" quite like wearing socks and sandals. I am sure T. S. Eliot must have done so from time to time.

Again, as an immature male, I tended to wear white socks until I was well past my teens. Now that I am a serious man, I favor dark socks, though, truth be told, I have never been able to successfully purchase a pair of socks for myself. Underwear sometimes; socks never. I now have a whole drawer full of slippery black socks that I purchased myself and that will not stay up. Only a woman knows how to buy men's socks.

Fortunately for me, Carolyn and the girls now buy me SmartWool socks. The heels and toes don't wear out quite so fast, they stay up, they keep my feet warm all winter, and they are perfect for wearing with sandals. Sure they look a trifle geriatric, but then more summers of my life have passed than are to come. I am now a serious older man. I should be able to pull them off —or on, as the case may be.

(A final note of caution: Nothing says "I am a silly and supercilious man" quite like being caught wearing nothing *but* socks. To stand naked before the world—not to mention the love of your life—wearing nothing but crew socks is an embarrassment to all living things. To spare yourself unwanted mortification, always remove your socks before your underwear. Seriously.)

# THE UNITED COLORS OF ME

Plum, I am told, is the new black, the go-to color for all occasions. I'm not sure I believe that, as I have not seen a lot of deep purple tuxedos around town, but then Maine tends to lag a year or ten behind the fashion curve. Be that as it may, color does reappear after a long chiaroscuro winter. There are purple and magenta primroses blossoming in the shade by the back steps, a flock of flaring yellow daffodils basks in the sun along the foundation, pink and purple pansies flutter in a pot on the back porch, the ruddy rhubarb starts to erupt, and the trees take on a faint blush as they bleed into bud. Then, bright yellow forsythia flags me down all over town.

Unless you count evergreen as a color, we are a color-starved people here in the Northeast. Perhaps that's why I'm drawn to concentrations of color—the lipstick red of the tulips in the neighbor's yard, the fiery blaze of a blackbird's wing, the cherry tomatoes in the Chip Chadbourn still-life above the kitchen table. Many of the things I love—flowers, birds, insects, art—are saturated with color, yet I myself am not a very colorful character. I live in a gray house, drive a navy blue car, and own a black dog. My wardrobe, such as it is, runs heavily to neutral and earth tones, a bit of green or blue here and there, but mostly shades of gray and brown.

I thought of all this this morning when I pulled a squash-yellow Yarmouth Clam Festival t-shirt over my head and was startled by its brightness. I quickly covered it up with a faded green sweatshirt, not wanting to call attention to myself. For the most part I'm a pretty drab guy, dirty blond hair going gray, strawberry blond beard gone silver and white, old khakis, faded jeans, shirts, sweaters, and jackets in mute stony tones.

Over the years there have been a few glaring exceptions to my colorless couture—a silk shirt the iridescent blue of a dragonfly's thorax, a gommy cotton cardigan a little too purple for its own good, a down jacket so salmony pink I'd have sooner eaten than worn it, and, still protesting its neglect in the sweater drawer, a baby blue v-neck so powdery and pastel I could only pull it off if I golfed and I don't. Maybe if I'd gone to UMO, but probably not even then.

It's hard for a man to wear bright or pretty colors (underwear and ties don't count) without looking flamboyant or fey. The primary exception to this rule is sport. Skiers and cyclists can get away with almost anything, though no one really looks good in wildly colorful, form-fitting bike gear. Team colors, however, are exempt from censure. I mean who but a Celtics fan could get away with wearing Kelly green in public? If you're wearing purple and gold, you'd better attend Cheverus High School, worship the Minnesota Vikings, or be a bishop or a king.

Even given the chromatic exemption for sports, however, I've always been thankful that the school colors of the high schools I've rooted for—Westbrook and Yarmouth—are blue and white. I'd have trouble donning anything red. Maroon's okay; red's just too blatant. And I've always felt sorry for kids who have to attend schools that deck themselves out in Halloween orange and black. Orange is a hard color to pull off unless you're a resident of a Buddhist monastery or a county jail.

When you come right down to it, Maine is pretty much black and white and green all over. Black bears, chickadees, snow, pine, spruce. The only orange accents are the daylilies. That's why there's no excuse for the new agriculture license plates, their gaudy sunset colors so at odds with the subdued character of the state. If you feel the need for more orange in your life, consider Tennessee.

# FALL

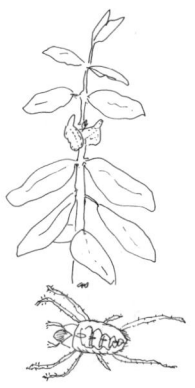

# UNDER MILKWEED

For the past week or ten days I have been spending odd
moments sitting in a bright blue Adirondack chair in
the back yard staring at the leggy, autumnal remains of
Carolyn's flower bed. The coneflowers with their drooping
white petals and elegant, spiky yellow cones are still in
pretty good shape, as are the sturdy pink clusters of the
Live Forever sedums, but the asters are bent and bowed and
the lowly melon pinks are turning to mulch on the ground.
Bumblebees still pry open the mouths of the lavender turtle-
heads, crawl inside, and emerge with hairy legs laden with
the golden pollen, but just about everything else has gone by.

    The sorriest looking plants in the garden are the five or
six stalks of milkweed that appeared unbidden and sought
clemency. Their oblong leaves are turning black and sooty
where they still exist at all. Most have been devoured right
down to the stem by scores of milkweed tiger moth caterpillars, those hairy little beings with showy tufts of black and
white and enormous appetites. Over the course of last few

weeks I watched as the gluttonous caterpillars arrived, small and meek, methodically gnawed away leaf after leaf, then departed bold and huge.

This time of year, primary school classrooms all over Greater Portland and Maine are witnessing the miraculous transformation of monarch caterpillars as they create their gold-leafed little green chrysalises, emerging after a time as brilliant orange and black butterflies bound for Mexico. Ordinarily we find a monarch or two on our milkweed, but this year the tiger moths must have been just too much for them, as they were for the critter I had been watching from my too-blue chair.

Back in the high summer of August, I discovered a common garden spider spinning her web between two stalks of milkweed. She was so large and bloated that when I pointed her out to members of my family they all gasped and took a step back. She looked like a brown strawberry hiding beneath a pair of milkweed leaves she had secured to one another with strands of silk. All day long she would hang upside down in her leafy chamber, one leg slightly exposed where she tended her trap. Each night she would eat her old web and weave a new one, an invisible-to-insects orb that would hold a small cricket or fly but not a bee.

Between phone calls and writings, I would repair to the chair and watch, hoping ghoulishly to witness a capture, but also transported by all the life pulsing around the web. When you first sit down in front of a plant, there can seem to be nothing going on, but even the slightest attention will quickly reveal an earnest and industrious natural drama. Ants and flies seem to be addicted to the milky sap on the surface of the milkweed and are everywhere. Honeybees and bumblebees harvesting pollen normally avoid the web, but when they blunder into it, they quickly extract themselves. I never once saw the spider venture out to bind her victims or suck their blood, but the evidence of her carnage was everywhere in her web, in her lair, and, if I poked around carefully, on the ground beneath.

Then the milkweed tiger moth caterpillars arrived and began dismantling the milkweed mouthful by mouthful. I somehow assumed that the great spider would feast upon their slow, soft feathery bodies, but they so outnumbered her that she must have given up. One morning a week or ten days ago I went outside to check her web and found it abandoned and in tatters. The very leaf she had hidden beneath for all those weeks was gone, stripped to its central vein by the caterpillars. I looked for days amidst the vegetation and the leaf litter for her new home, but she was gone. As I searched for the missing spider, I began to sense that it must have been some similar episode of arachnid disappointment that led E. B. White to write *Charlotte's Web,* his rueful celebration of the life cycle of a barn spider.

I had hoped to see a hatch of spiderlings depart the milkweed, but wherever the spider went, she seems to have taken her immortality with her. Today, there is nothing left of the milkweed except the stalk and the pods. Yet even there on those forlorn, testicular pods there is life. I would have mistaken it for mold spores had not Carolyn pointed out that the tiny orange polyps have legs. They are, in fact, aphids. And what business they have to transact on the remains of the milkweed is yet to be seen.

Now, upon closer inspection, I see that some fantastic little creature has deposited a coppery egg capsule atop the denuded stalk for my viewing enjoyment. So when the relentless bad news from around the world gets to be too much for me, I can repair to the back yard and watch life go on oblivious to our human failings.

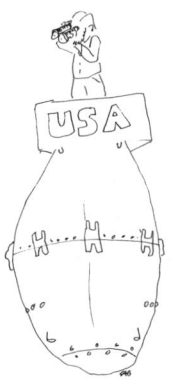

# THREAT ASSESSMENT

Bear with me, won't you, while I attempt to allay my own fears. Whether it is my advancing age, the fact that I have sent grown children out into this perilous world, or a truly elevated threat to our national security and our survival as a species, I find myself experiencing more anxiety about the future these days than at any time in all my years on Earth. I have a strange feeling, however, that things are no worse now than they have ever been for homo sapiens Americanus.

I started thinking the good old days weren't necessarily all that good awhile back as I read the World War II diaries of a Portland businessman. I was amazed to find that he detested FDR as much as I dislike GWB. His Roosevelt animus had to do with his perception that FDR was a liar and anti-business. My Bush complex stems from the fact that I see him as a liar and too pro-business. The more things change. . . .

And you think we're on high alert now?  Forget airport baggage checks, this gentleman was spending three hours a night in the Portland Observatory on Munjoy Hill watching for German subs in Casco Bay. At least I'm not worried about Al Qaeda fighters sneaking ashore on Cousins Island tonight.

This awful war in Iraq and the tangentially related war on terrorism are threatening to take all the fun out of life, but, come to think of it, I grew up fearing the Red Menace and the A-bomb, practicing air-raid drills at school, and wondering why our family didn't have a bomb shelter. The threat was just as real when I was ten, just more abstract and remote.

These days, we all wonder whether that static on the phone line is the National Security Agency listening in, but Big Brother paranoia is nothing new in the land of the free and the home of the brave. Back in the 1960s, it was the FBI doing the illegal domestic surveillance, keeping tabs on civil rights activists and antiwar protesters. I appreciate the Maine Public Utilities Commission asking Verizon to pinky swear it didn't turn over all our phone records to the government, but I have to believe that whenever the white shirts of the NSA, FBI, and CIA show up at their door, the phone company execs poop will their pants and do whatever they were asked.

On the environmental front, it now seems as though we may run out of time before we run out of oil, what with global warming, climate change, holes in the ozone, and dead zones in the oceans. But, hey, we've been on this course all of my life. Forty years ago, we were warned that we had to do something about overpopulation, but I haven't heard a word about ZPG (zero population growth) in years.

Of course, it's hard to convince anyone in Maine that the

world is overpopulated when you can drive five hours north and not see anything other than trees, road kill, and the occasional deer. That, too, may be about to change if the plunderers of Plum Creek manage to get permission from the Land Use Regulation Commission to turn Moosehead Lake into Jackson Hole East, in the process transforming their vast holdings of cheap, under-taxed forest lands into $100,000 house lots.

But then there's always been some crackpot carpetbagger with a get-rich-quick scheme for the wilds of Maine. Remember the Passamaquoddy Tidal Power project in the 1930s? The Dickey-Lincoln hydropower plan in the 1960s? The Pittston Oil Refinery in the 1970s? Well, we didn't build Quoddy, we didn't flood Aroostook County, we still don't refine oil in Machiasport as far as I know, and I'm betting we're not going to turn Moosehead Lake into a condo resort, either.

Make no mistake about it, the new threats to our security are real, but then security has always been an illusion. The threats to the environment are real too, but no more real than they have ever been. And the threats to democracy and freedom—whether from imperial presidents or fanatical foreigners—are all too real and persistent; they're just nothing new.

Look at it this way. If you were born in the 1980s or 1990s, these are the good old days. Gee, I'm starting to feel better already.

# HOW STUPID AM I?

The recent high school open house left me feeling exhausted and overwhelmed, my head spinning with things I haven't thought about in forty years, if then. Stoichiometry. Colligative properties. The emission spectra of atoms. Mercantile Theory. Logarithms as an inverse function. Asymptotic behavior. Holy slide rule! What time is recess?

I vaguely recall high school, which I attended from 1963 to 1967, as being relatively easy. I also seem to recall being fairly bright—National Honor Society, top ten in my class, etc. After previewing daughter Tess's junior-year program, however, I seriously wonder whether, if I returned to high school today, I could even graduate, let alone make the honor roll. I came home asking myself, "How stupid am I?"

I might possibly be able to help Tess with her English and U.S. History homework, but other than that she's on her own. I'm amazed that she manages to assimilate all this knowledge while maintaining a busy year-round sports schedule, but apparently it can be done, as she and most of her teammates are honor students. The fact that I couldn't do it at fifty-eight forces me to conclude that my daughter is smarter than I am at this point.

"It's pretty intense," is all Tess said when I asked her about her academic load.

Certainly, we all want to give our children the best possible chances "to create fulfilling lives in a changing world" (from the Yarmouth School Department motto), but sometimes I wonder whether the pressures and demands we place on them are wise or warranted. We don't push Tess; she pushes herself. Still, high school these days seems far more competitive than it was when I was in school.

Back then, the majority of the 222 kids in my class did not go to college. Most went to work. Some went into the military. Those of us who were going on to college took the SATs, applied to one or two schools, and attended whichever one we got into and could afford. There were no whirlwind junior-year college tours, no SAT prep classes, no Advanced Placement courses and exams, no hiring private college counselors, and no applying to five or ten colleges, as seems to be the norm these days.

The role of the parent has changed as well. It's not just shepherding your kid around New England, the Northeast, or the entire country shopping for the right college; it's the level of personal involvement with schooling. Maybe we had parent-teacher conferences in the '60s, but I don't recall my parents being at the high school as often as I am—for open houses, student-led conferences, code nights, games, ceremonies, etc., etc.

When I was in school, my parents got to see how I was doing four times a year when I brought home my report card. Today, I can log on to PowerSchool to check Tess's progress and performance daily. Sometimes, I know how she did on a test before she does. Naturally, I like to think that I am being an involved and supportive father, but I also understand why Tess often wishes I'd just mind my own damn business.

My sense of being overwhelmed by the prospect of her schoolwork obviously has something to do with having lost a great many brain cells over the past forty years, but if I am not as smart as I was at seventeen, I have to believe I am a little wiser. And if the true end of education is wisdom, as I believe it is, I seriously question the value of placing such an intense emphasis on academic achievement.

My own experience has taught me a number of lessons that are not taught in our high-performing high schools. I don't mean to undermine an educational enterprise I have invested a great deal of time in supporting, but here's the truth of the gray matter as I know it:

Ninety percent of what you learn in high school and college you'll never need to know again. Students on the honor roll do not live more fulfilling lives than those who are not. The smartest kids in a class don't necessarily get the best grades. The two wealthiest people I know did not go to college at all. Education is not a competition. Learning should be fun and pursued for its own sake. There is no correlation at all between intelligence and happiness.

How was school today, honey?

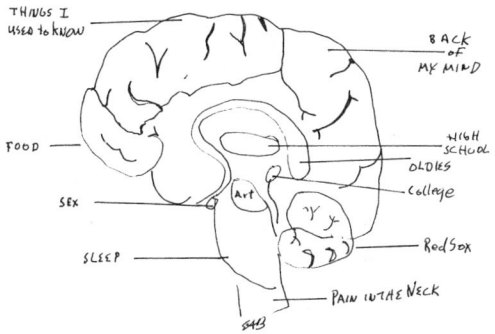

# DOWN MEMORY LAME

The other day, for reasons that don't bear repeating, I was trying to remember the route I walked to junior high school forty-odd years ago. I can remember virtually every step and turn of the long walk I made each day to high school for three years until my buddy Christopher got a car and started picking me up, but I cannot remember how I got to junior high, who I walked with, or whether I might have ridden my bike. I'm pretty sure I never rode a school bus in my life, but I can't swear to it. Strange to think that you could have done something 350 times (175 school days in both seventh and eighth grade) without remembering a thing about it, but then I've always had a spotty memory and it's getting worse.

Names have always been a problem for me, and, knowing this, Carolyn has grown accustomed to my failure to introduce her at public gatherings and social functions. It's not that I'm impolite; it's just that I often can't remember the names of people I know very well. Truth be told, I have even forgotten Carolyn's name on a few occasions, more out of introduction anxiety than forgetfulness.

What I'm going to remember and what I'm not and why is a total mystery to me. Most of the time I find this random access memory more amusing than troubling, but it does present a few professional and personal problems. For instance, having written about a thousand words a day for thirty-odd years, I constantly worry that I might have written something before without remembering it. I'm pretty sure I have mentioned my poor memory in print at other times, but have I mentioned that there are certain things I have never been able to commit to memory even when I've tried? For example, I cannot remember, no matter how hard I try, where the knife, fork, and spoon go when setting the table or whether the shutter opening is faster, slower, larger, or smaller when the f-stop numbers get bigger. This is embarrassing for a guy who writes about photography every month in an international photojournalism magazine.

I am reminded of my absentmindedness nightly at 10:00 P.M. when I take my daily medicine—three pills, two for blood pressure, one for bladder function. I never forget to take my medicine, but several times a week I forget whether I have already taken the pills or not. Carolyn got me one of those weekly pill dispensers designed for forgetful old folks like myself, but then I'd forget to fill it. So now we're back to "Honey, do you remember whether I've taken my medicine or not?"

I can understand how I might lose track of something so repetitive, but I find it extraordinary that there are whole years missing from my memory. With a little bit of prompting from friends or family, I can sometimes conjure up specific events and incidents, but there are many times when even that doesn't help. Carolyn insisted recently, for instance, that ten or fifteen years ago we attended a big birthday party for a friend at a restaurant in the Old Port, but try as I might I could not recall ever having been in that restaurant.

Obviously, some of these memory lapses are related to aging. When I was in high school and college, I committed entire plays by Edward Albee, Harold Pinter, and Brendan Behan to memory, but these days I have trouble helping daughter Tess memorize passages from Whitman and Shakespeare or the Preamble to the Constitution.

When I was a kid, I played a lot of baseball, and some guys I know remember every play of every game they ever played. But I can only remember two or three moments from all those games I played—a ball I hit over the fence in Little League All-Star batting practice, the moment I realized I had pitched a one-hitter, and racing back to catch a long fly ball only to discover that, because there was no fence in the outfield, I had caught a home run.

But the breakdown of brain chemistry doesn't explain everything. I also have to believe I have just stopped trying to remember a lot of things. I have watched every World Series since 1957, for instance, and there was a time when I could tell you who played, who won, and what their lineups were, if not the scores. Now I just enjoy the moment and let the action slide across my retina and disappear into the electrochemical vagaries of my brain never to be seen again. I'm pretty sure, however, that I'll remember who won the 2004 World Series.

There was something else I was going to mention here, something about having to write everything down, but now I can't remember what it was.

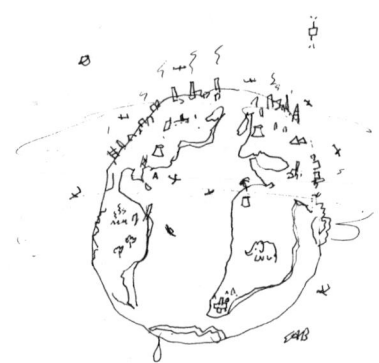

# THE DIMMING OF PLANET EARTH

In case you hadn't heard, the polar ice caps are melting at an alarming rate. Polar bears are drowning in their search for sea ice from which to hunt seals. Soon they will be competing for garbage with the black bears at the Greenville dump. Glaciers are melting all over the world. Holes in the ozone layer are allowing the sun to sauté us alive. Global warming is a scientific fact. If you don't believe it, you're a dinosaur. But then we're all dinosaurs, aren't we? And we're following those dear, dim creatures into oblivion.

I had never heard of global *dimming*, however, until last week when PBS aired a NOVA documentary entitled *Dimming the Sun.* Apparently, we *Dino sapiens* have managed to pump enough particulate matter into the atmosphere since the 1950s to decrease the amount of sunlight reaching the Earth by anywhere from 10 to 30 percent, depending upon where you live.

One of the surprising contributors to dimming appears to be contrails from jets that, under the right meteorological conditions, seed clouds and expand wildly. This was demonstrated on September 12, 2001, when, with all civilian and commercial aviation grounded, scientists took advantage of the momentarily clear skies to determine that just six military jets flying between Virginia and Pennsylvania managed to create enough exhaust to shade 7,700 square miles.

As with everything these days, there's good news and bad news on the global dimming front. The good news is that we have managed to reduce air pollution by as much as 50 percent over the past thirty years. The bad news is that global dimming had apparently been cooling the Earth. Now, clearer skies are accelerating global warming.

Sooner or later, you and I and the folks next door are going to have to face the fact that we are destroying this planet, but I don't see any signs of recognition just yet. We go right on tooling around town in our evil-doer autos, cranking up the oil-fired furnace when the temperature drops below sixty-five, plugging in desktops, laptops, iPods, cell phones, and flatscreen TVs (not to mention toasters, washing machines, dryers, dishwashers, microwaves and a host of other unnecessary appliances), and jetting off to Belize or the Turks and Caicos for a little fun in the obscured sun. We seem unable or unwilling to do anything substantial about our pathological lifestyles. As a pack-a-day smoker, I understand denial all too well.

What I do not understand is why no one seems to be asking us to make the necessary changes in our wasteful ways. Oh sure, there's a push every once in awhile to get us to use energy-saver light bulbs, but I'm pretty sure we're not going to make any serious improvement in our damaged environment just by turning off the lights when we leave the room.

What we need are radical changes in our behaviors and our expectations. We need to start making sacrifices before we sacrifice Planet Earth. Government has a role to play, but what it's really going to take is a sea change in consciousness. To that end, allow me to suggest a few reforms that might help clear the air before the lights go out on Planet Earth entirely:

1. Get rid of your second car. Better yet, get rid of your first.
2. Get rid of any vehicle that doesn't get at least 50 MPG.
3. Tax parking lots at a higher rate than waterfront property.
4. Tax energy use more heavily than real estate.
5. Tax second homes more heavily than primary residences.
6. Don't develop any undeveloped land.
7. Don't fly except in emergencies.
8. Don't eat any food that is grown, raised, caught, or produced more than a hundred miles from where you live.
9. Don't have more than two children.
10. Stop invading oil-producing nations.

# THERE IS ALWAYS A FALL

We had a rather fickle summer this year, a few fragments of
fair beach weather bracketed by one authentic heat wave, a
strange period of almost tropical humidity, rumors of rain,
and a lot of days that rightly belonged in other seasons. Now
I hear we're supposed to be in for another rugged, old-
fashioned winter—soul-chilling temperatures and deep
snows—but I wouldn't bet on it. We're just as apt to have
an open winter, which is no winter at all, unless, of course,
you like to skate. In my close to sixty years, I have observed
that there are years without summer, years without spring,
and years without winter, but there is always a fall.

As I write this, a tropical storm is starting to shake herself off like a wet dog, sprinkling the yard with the first
downed leaves and irregular showers that smell of Carolina's
Outer Banks. But I have every confidence that, come tomor-
row, we will be back into the regulation-issue autumn
weather—cool, crisp, sunny sweater weather—that makes
fall the favored season of so many people I know.

You'd think that fall, marking as it does the down cycle of the wheeling seasons, the late middle age of the year as it heads for the dead of winter, might be a depressing time, yet more people of my acquaintance, myself included, find spring the anxious time of year. Fall, for all its intimations of mortality, is stable, dependable, fresh—a deep cleansing breath before the inevitable.

Since I first discovered John Updike in high school (his revelation to me being that suburban life could be the stuff of literature), I have not passed an autumn without thinking of the first line of his fine short story "In Football Season": "Do you remember a fragrance girls acquire in autumn?" I knew exactly what he meant when I first read the story at sixteen, having gratefully inhaled those wafts of lemony musk that rise from young women wrapped in wool. But girls don't smell like that anymore. Gone are the girls of fall 1965 with their Jackie Kennedy flips, culottes, cardigans, and stadium coats. Girls these days are, thankfully, no longer on the sidelines watching but out there on the playing fields creating a more egalitarian aroma of perspiration and health.

Another essence of past falls you don't smell much anymore is the pleasantly acrid aroma of burning leaves. An e-mail correspondent (something that didn't exist in 1965) called this to my attention last week, writing to ask whether families rake up leaves anymore so the kids can jump in them and then burn them in the gutter. I suppose she thought I'd know because, safe behind this screen of printed words, I pretend to know everything when, in fact, I know very little about the ways of the world.

But, yes, there will be a pile of leaves again this year, perhaps two, both about the size of compact cars. Like mounds of yellow, orange and red potato chips, they will be high, light, whole and crisp unless the neighborhood kids start jumping in them, quickly reducing the piles to mulch. I miss my girls jumping in the leaves. At seventeen, Tess may or may not be too old to jump in the leaves, but I wish she would anyway. She would not, however, disappear into the musty depths as she did just a few falls back. At five feet, five inches, she is too long and bony to retreat into complete innocence much longer.

We will not be burning any leaves on the roadside though. I'd love to send them skyward as burnt offerings to the ozone gods, but I suppose we shouldn't and so we won't. As Earth tilts on its axis, starving the leaves of sunlight, they will blush their respective colors and fall to the ground. We will rake them up and drag them on an old tarp out into the woods where we will spread them over the bare roots along the footpath in hopes of creating a little more earth beneath our feet.

## COMMON GROUND

Over the fourth weekend of September, almost the entire population of the City of Portland (pop. 64,000) headed north to the small town of Unity (pop. 1,936), there to turn pastures into parking lots and the dusty old Unity Fairgrounds into the Maine Organic Farmers & Gardeners Association's annual Common Ground Fair. After a Woodstock-like mudfest in '06, the fair was a huge success the following year. The gorgeous weekend weather attracted a record-breaking 62,000 souls to what *Down East* magazine has called "Maine's most authentic country fair, uniting as it does old-time folkways with progressive ideas about living the good life on a fragile planet." (Please forgive the above indulgence, but this is the first time in forty years of journalism that I have had the opportunity to quote myself and I couldn't resist. I wouldn't have done so except that MOFGA uses the quote from my September 2000 *Down East* article about Common Ground on its web site, albeit without attribution.)

By the time we arrived at Common Ground on Sunday afternoon, several of the local food vendors had sold out and closed up tent, and the lines at those food booths that were still open were long and slow. We probably spent fifteen minutes waiting to order paper plates of bland, tasteless chicken masala and rice. I'm guessing the Indian chefs had run out of spices.

The rag-tag tribe of aging hippies, political and environmental activists, organic farmers, and wannabe country folk munched blooming onions and falafel gyros and sipped cider and lemonade as they milled around the near treeless fairground, checking out everything under the sun from Native American basketry to New Age cosmetics, along the way picking up bumper stickers that urged everything from freeing Tibet and Cuba to ending the war in Iraq. (Never thought to ask how to free Tibet without invading it.)

At Common Ground there were more dreadlocks, tie-dyed t-shirts, sandals, and bare feet in one place in Maine than there have been since the Phish concert in Limestone in '98. There were also a handful of handy folks of the sort who would survive a meteor strike or a nuclear blast, resourceful individualists who can still take to the woods, grow food, make boats, sleds, snowshoes, and create heat and light from sun, wind, garden waste, and manure.

Farmers, organic and otherwise, are becoming something of a curiosity as rural Maine becomes increasingly suburbanized. Some 65 percent of Maine residents now live in areas designated by the U.S. Census as metropolitan or "micropolitan." Virtually everything south of Bangor is suburban. This being so, country fairs, organic and otherwise, are becoming zoos, places denatured twenty-first-century people can go seasonally to be reminded how vegetables grow and animals smell.

Our relationship with nature is now tenuous at best. Busloads of school kids, for instance, were trucked to the Cumberland Fair last week to see and sometimes touch chickens, ducks, rabbits, goats, sheep, pigs, horses, and cows, but anxious parents and chaperones secretly worried about things like bird flu, salmonella, and e. coli.

"Don't put your hands in the horse's mouth, Darlene."

Horse pulling is still a popular attraction (and one of my guilty pleasures) at the fairs, but, as the number of teamsters working the woods with horses dwindles (and animal rights activists complain), I have to wonder how much longer huge draft animals will be hauling those blocks of cement up and down the dirt floors of the pulling barns. And now that the Cumberland Fair has added the extreme sport of bull riding to its agricultural attractions, the horse pull may soon go the way of the girlie show. (The Cumberland Fair, c. 1963, was the first place I ever saw an entirely naked woman. It wasn't a pretty sight.)

Attending the fairs, I get the impression that farming has become a marginal, often nonprofit venture, a once vital part of the Maine landscape and economy now propped up by a few niche markets and a lot of local preservation groups. Think Wolfe's Neck and Pineland Farm.

Inspired by the trip to Common Ground and determined to do my small part to support local farmers, I stopped by the farmers' market that pops up on Thursday afternoons in the parking lot of the Catholic church. I purchased a bunch of carrots grown by our church sexton and a big, yellow heirloom tomato grown bio-dynamically by an old college friend. Sure I paid a little more for homegrown veggies, but it was worth it.

If you eat a steady diet of cheap plastic supermarket produce trucked in from California, Florida, and Chile, you tend to forget that carrots and tomatoes can taste as sweet as the Maine earth from which they came.

# PICTURES OF CAROLYN

My favorite picture of my wife Carolyn is a fading black-and-white enlargement of a snapshot I took twenty-nine years ago. It stands here on the windowsill behind the computer in a dusty plastic cube and I look at it every day as I write.

In the photograph, Carolyn is twenty-three years old, the same age as our daughter Nora, a year younger than our daughter Hannah. Her eyes are closed because I am a lousy photographer, but her closed eyes give her a dreamy, faraway look that seems to grow more lovely and romantic as the years pass.

That photograph was taken in our Portland apartment on the evening of February 22, 1980. I know this because it was both my birthday and the night the Cinderella U.S. Olympic hockey team defeated the dreaded Russians on their way to the gold medal. We had a few close friends over for a dinner party, ate lots of poached salmon, drank lots of white wine, and talked about the future until the wee hours. There is an empty bottle and an empty wine glass on the table in front of Carolyn and she is either talking or laughing, probably both.

We were proverbially young and foolish that night, penniless but full of potential. Carolyn was finishing college. I was finishing an unsuccessful novel. A few months later, on October 9, 1980, we would be married in Winchester, England. By the time we got home Hannah was on the way. Life began in earnest. Forget fiction. I got a job on a newspaper to help pay the bills. Nora arrived. We bought a house. Carolyn got a part-time Christmas job at L.L. Bean that turned into a career. Tess was born ten years after Hannah. Now she's in high school. Carolyn went to graduate school. Hannah and Nora just graduated from college themselves. Now we are celebrating our twenty-fifth wedding anniversary, and those twenty-five years passed in about the same amount of time it took to write this paragraph.

I've known Carolyn since she was fifteen, almost the same age as Tess. I've loved her since she was twenty-three. She has now been married to me longer than she has not. So there are pictures of Carolyn all over my little sunroom office. There's a snapshot someone took just before I entered her life, another of her at the lake, and a little picture of her sitting cross-legged on the floor, pouting and pregnant, her hair longer than it has been in years. On the bulletin board over the desk is a picture of her with short hair, sitting on the floor with Hannah and Nora on Christmas morning 1985. The photo is mounted in a blue macaroni frame one of the girls must have made. There's also a Christmas 1997 photograph of all the Beem girls—Carolyn, my mother, our three girls, their Aunt Marji, and cousin Emily—wearing vintage ladies' dress hats. The original of my favorite photograph is tucked into the frame of the bulletin board where it has been for more than twenty years.

On my desk itself there are three pictures of Carolyn. In the most colorful one she wearing a green and gold fleece hat Marji made for her, along with a bright yellow parka and purple fleece scarf. I took that photograph a couple of years ago at a cross-country ski meet. Beside the winter portrait is a photograph of Carolyn and our daughters taken at Nora's graduation from Smith. The most recent photograph I have of Carolyn is clipped to a clear Plexiglas clipboard behind the phone. It is the photograph that prompted me to write this column about the love of my life rather than about my latest complaint.

This new picture of Carolyn was taken at her Uncle Alton and Aunt Fran's fiftieth wedding anniversary party in Freeport. In it she is wearing the dangling earrings Nora brought back for her from Belize. Her face is sunny and tanned, her impossibly dark brown eyes fixed on me. But it is the expression on her face that causes me to smile every time I glance at it. It is an expression of amusement, of tolerance, just the trace of a girlish smirk crossing the face of a wise and beautiful woman. I suppose Carolyn looks wise to me because I know she's wise to me. I feel summed up, contained, and approved of in that lovely look on her face. Now I'm off to buy her an anniversary present, but that look of love is the only gift I want or need.

Happy anniversary, sweetheart.

# DOWNTOWN IN THE DAY

The evening sky turned sulfurous yellow for an hour last week. Strange, otherworldly. It was like the light of the past shining briefly on the present, so I took a walk down Congress Street forty-some years ago.

I was on my way to Ruthie Baker's Recordland to sift through the bins of LPs looking for a new Joan Baez album, but first I ducked down the stairs to the subterranean cavern of Pinetree Billiards to have a smoke, watch the local hustlers, and get in the proper frame of mind, which at that time was high school bohemian.

Across the square in the Libby Building, which would eventually have to come down to make way for I. M. Pei's Portland Museum of Art, Ocy Downs was drilling music into one of her piano students. Just down the hall, Doris Rankin, who would die in her sleep after an evening of Scrabble, was teaching girls to type and take shorthand at Gray's Portland Business School.

In the lobby of the Congress Square Hotel, Barney Zade,

who would hire me to drive a cab a few years later, was dispatching Town Taxis to Bramhall, Union Station, and the West End. There were dead men driving all over town that evening, but, fortunately, I do not believe in ghosts.

Eternally old Mr. Campbell, a friendly gentleman with a scholar's stoop, stood in the window of his bookstore. He smiled and nodded, making me feel guilty that I bought most of my books across the street at Jones Book Store. I was dating owner Leo Boyle's daughter Terry at the time and she had just given me Dylan Thomas's *Collected Poems* for Christmas.

There were a lot of people downtown for a weekday, shoppers crisscrossing Congress Street from Porteous to Owen-Moore, suburban matrons checking out the latest fashions at Oscar Benoit's, teenagers headed for Prep Hall at A. H. Benoit's down off Monument Square. I wondered whether Benoit's still gave out Benno Bucks. Probably, because people were still collecting S & H Green Stamps and redeeming them at Plaidland.

The really sharp urban ladies would be down the street at Bernie's Fashions or getting their hair done at Sebastian's Coiffures by a brilliantined werewolf.

So I stopped in to see Ruthie Baker, who was as close to hip as anything in Portland, and bought the new Joan Baez, but not before fretting about whether to buy Tim Hardin or Dave Van Ronk instead. I was a real folkie "in the day," as they say now.

Before heading back to the present I figured I'd get a bite to eat. Lots of choices—The Splendid, The Puritan, Your Host, Bentley's —all plain-vanilla downtown restaurants of the sort you only find in Manhattan these days. You want something different, try Cathay Garden. But I wasn't that hungry, so I settled for a BLT at Charley's on the Square where, fifteen years later, I'd eat every day while working at Portland Public Library.

Right next door was the Surplus Store, a great place for an antiwar adolescent to buy army gear. If you wanted real bell-bottoms, this was the place. I figured the Surplus Store would last forever. Cheap and durable never goes out of style. When I went back and looked today, however, the sign was still there but the store was suddenly empty.

As far as I can tell, in fact, the only business that's still where it was in 1966 is Springer's Jewelers. That's what Portland's like though, isn't it? It always looks the same, but it's not.

# THE CASE FOR OPTIMISM

Optimists come in a variety of types, from cheerful to cock-eyed, cautious to eternal. Whether they just want to be optimistic or they just can't help it, the one thing all optimists have in common, God bless 'em, is a redemptive view of the world. Things could be worse. Things will get better.

Lately, I've been feeling that I ought to be more optimistic myself. Not that I really believe optimism is warranted given the sorry state of world affairs and the human condition, but I'm beginning to think that my relentlessly pessimistic (albeit totally realistic) view of the world isn't doing me or anyone around me much good. Intellectually, I understand that you can change the world simply by the way you look at it. Attitude is everything. Practically, however, I've never been much good at changing my mind.

Basically, I look at the world pretty much the same way I did when I was sixteen—critically. And I tend to view people whose views have changed, i.e., become more moderate or conservative, as they mature as sell-outs. I'm an idealist, so

I like to think of my extremely critical nature as an agent of change. I criticize everything—from politics to the arts, education to athletics—in the hope that pointing out what's wrong will help to improve things. Come to think of it, that's pretty optimistic in and of itself, maybe even a bit naïve. And it certainly doesn't make the people who have to listen to my endlessly pessimistic assessments feel any better.

I've been thinking about the prospect of reforming my sour disposition ever since I had a conversation with an extremely sanguine Scotsman a few weeks back. When, in the course of interviewing the gentleman about his distinguished career in photography, I asked him how he had managed to maintain such a positive outlook in his work over the course of more than fifty years, I was quite taken aback when he told me he believes we are now living at the best possible time in the history of the world. Hunh?! What about war and terrorism, religious and political extremism, natural disasters and incipient diseases, economic injustice, and environmental degradation?

"Nothing we can't handle," the old gent replied in a soft Scottish burr.

Having grown up during World War II, he explained, he remembered when bombs rained down on his hometown every night for three months. Nothing's been that bad since. What are a few random terrorist attacks compared to an all-out, round-the-clock world war? What's Al Qaeda compared to the Nazis? Is the long-term threat of global warming really any more frightful than the cold war threat of instant nuclear annihilation? Things could be worse. Things will get better.

When I got off the phone with the gentleman, I was

smiling. I felt lighter, happier, more optimistic than I had felt in years. The uplift didn't last much past the evening news, but I did begin right there and then trying to look beyond our present situation—unpopular war, unpopular president, huge budget deficits, zero environmental enforcement, etc.—toward the certainty that this too shall pass.

Now I'm starting to think that there may be a next chapter in the American saga after all. Maybe an honest and wise leader—possibly a woman—will emerge from the next generation to inspire the cowering masses to new greatness. Maybe the crises in the Middle East that erupt into terrorism and fanaticism will resolve themselves in some astonishingly simple ways. Then maybe Americans will be free to turn their attentions to cracking down on corporate polluters, developing clean alternative energy sources, caring for the poor, and exporting peace and freedom rather than war and fear. Nothing we can't handle.

After a decade of conservative repression, the backlash from the Bush years could very well make the sixties seem as tame as a Boy Scout jamboree. I can almost feel the Dionysian rush of liberty and justice for all right now. Gee, it feels good to be optimistic for a change!

# WORDS FAIL ME

As I approach retirement age with no prospects of ever retiring, I am more or less resigned to my own failure as a writer. Oh, I'm eternally grateful that I am able to eke out a modest living with words, but it's pretty clear that I will never attain my youthful goal. The conspicuously unpublished novels and unproduced screenplays may one day find publishers and producers, but it's clearly too late to achieve my one great literary ambition—to become a *New Yorker* writer.

Since college in the 1960s, I have regarded the *New Yorker* as the last bastion of sanity and quality in a world awash in irrational pap. For years, I sought counsel with great *New Yorker* writers to little or no avail.

In the early 1970s, I confess I stalked John Updike all over Ipswich, Massachusetts, dying to meet the man who managed to make the suburban reality I knew the stuff of literature. The great man was putting up storm windows the day I finally pulled into his driveway on Labor in Vain Road and introduced myself. In that brief driveway conversation, I felt I had been anointed.

"I hope to become a writer," I told Updike.

"You will," he replied, as though he recognized a kindred spirit.

A decade later, however, my hero obviously didn't remember me when, after I had become a staff writer for *Maine Times,* he turned me down for an interview. But then, hey, I've been turned down by the best. Over the course of a checkered forty-year career in journalism, I have only been turned down for interviews by four people—Updike, novelist John Fowles, socialite Brooke Astor, and essayist E. B. White, a pretty prestigious set of rejections, if I do say so myself.

The first time I wrote to E. B. White, it was to invite him to speak or read at Portland Public Library in 1976.

"My platform life is nonexistent," Mr. White wrote back. "This cuts me out of meeting some good people and visiting interesting places. But I live with it."

The second approach I made to the famously reclusive writer was a request for a *Maine Times* interview in 1983.

"My days of being interviewed are over," Mr. White replied, adding stylishly and poignantly, "along with a lot of other days."

Subsequently, I went on a long, successful run of collecting *New Yorker* writers, profiling as many as I could find who had Maine connections—baseball writer Roger Angell (E. B. White's stepson), novelist and short story writer Ann Beattie, miniaturist Nicholson Baker, memoirist Ved Mehta, and John McPhee, the king of long-form journalists. By virtue of the fact that photographer Bill Curtsinger here in Yarmouth had collaborated on a book with McPhee, we got to spend a night with him at his home in Princeton, New Jersey.

So anyway, I was feeling rather collegial about *New Yorker* writers when I ran into two of them at John Cole's memorial service a few years back. It could have been a double coup, but instead it turned into a double *fou*.

Novelist and nature writer Peter Matthiessen, the contemporary writer I admire most, had just come out with a wonderful new book about cranes. So when I ran into him at the reception after the service, I told him how very much I enjoyed *Birds of Paradise*.

"*Birds of Heaven*," Mr. Matthiessen corrected me. And that was pretty much the end of that conversation.

Across the reception room at the Daniel Snow Inn in Brunswick, I spotted humorist and food writer Calvin Trillin, who had just published a very funny novel about parking in Manhattan. I hurried to tell Mr. Trillin that I had gotten a real kick out of—uh-oh, it was happening again.

"*Tepper Isn't Going Out?*" Mr. Trillin prompted, and then he hurried off in pursuit of a fresh tray of canapés.

Not only am I a failure, I'm failing. Words fail me. That's why when, a couple of years ago, I spotted a gentleman hailing a cab in Manhattan who looked a lot like novelist Philip Roth (the man, not the taxi), I did not approach. I really wanted to know, however, whether it was indeed the author of *Portnoy's Complaint,* so I simply hollered, "Hey, Phil!"—much to the chagrin of my lovely wife Carolyn.

Sure enough, the tall, gaunt New Yorker craned his authorial head to see who was hailing him. I looked around, too, as of to say it wasn't me.

Hey, Phil? Was that the best I could do? I guess I should

be thankful it wasn't Woody Allen on that street corner. I can only imagine what sort of fool I would have made of myself.

# LISTEN TO THE NIGHT

The cold, clear, still air of approaching winter carries on its shivering wavelengths the strange and familiar sounds of night. The woods behind the house sound positively haunted at times, what with the wild calls of unseen coyotes and owls and the blood-curdling howls of the pack of hounds who inhabit the farm on the edge of town.

Closer to home, the darkened yard and the woods just beyond the garden, asleep beneath a blanket of leaves, are alive with rustlings. Mice and voles scuttering in the leaf litter and duff sound as large as skunks and coons once the moon rises. In the morning there will be deer hoofprints in the mud, but the hunted whitetails are silent and unseen.

Indoors, the night sounds are mostly mechanical—the hum of the refrigerator, the hushed roar of the furnace, the intermittent grinding of the sump pump as the frost drives groundwater into the basement, the drip-drip-drip of the leaky faucet in the bathroom, the periodic creak and groan of the girls' beds upstairs as they turn over in their sleep.

I don't sleep well. I'm up every two hours, three if I'm lucky, four if I'm ill. I lie in bed and listen to the night, trying to sort out the external sounds from those that only exist inside my head. I watch light shows with my eyes closed, glancing up at the clock every once in awhile to reestablish conscious connection—2:40, 4:20, 5:45, 6:10, time to get up. I go to bed exhausted and wake up exhausted. It's been that way for years now.

There was a time when I slept more peacefully, or at least was less fitful when awake at night. The other day, driving up High Street in Portland, I glanced over at the front windows of Number 72, my grandmother's old house, and suddenly remembered a night fifty years ago when, asleep on a rollaway cot in Nana Gibson's living room, I awoke to voices outside that very window. It was past midnight and the idea that people were still up and about at that time of night made me want to live in Portland when I grew up. (We were living in Massachusetts at the time.) It is comforting, even consoling to know that life goes on as you sleep.

That memory of listening to voices when I was seven prompted another memory of awaking perhaps a decade ago to the sounds of silence in Manhattan. I was staying on the Bowery in a friend's loft, the wild and wired sounds of the city three stories below. But at 4:00 A.M., I awoke from a sound sleep to an unexpected quiet as the city that never sleeps took a catnap before dawn. The silence was broken shortly by the rude noise of a garbage truck making its early morning rounds.

Eight or ten years ago, I was asleep in a tent on the banks of the Allagash when I woke up to the pre-dawn rumble of a logging truck just beyond the beauty strip. Rather than being annoyed, I felt reassured, knowing that even as I lay there in my sleeping bag, someone might hear me if I called out in the night. Miles above me, a nearly silent jet passed overhead, hundreds of people asleep in the sky as I lay awake in the woods.

Now I listen for the welcome sounds that herald the end of night—the *shirr* of car tires as the delivery man pulls up to drop off the morning newspaper, the first chirping of the early birds, the purposeful ticking of the heat returning to the baseboards, the hissing in my ears that is just the sound of me growing old.

# ON THANKSGIVING

When Tess mentioned the other day that Thanksgiving was her favorite holiday, I must admit I was a bit surprised. I thought Christmas, with its outpouring of gifts, must be every child's favorite holiday. When I asked her why, she said, "The food."

"But there's lots of food on Christmas Day, too," I pointed out, wondering whether she wasn't getting enough to eat.

"Preparing the food," Tess added, suggesting to me that what she likes about Thanksgiving is what I like about Thanksgiving—the gathering of the family to prepare and share a bountiful meal.

When I was a kid, we usually had Thanksgiving dinner at my grandparents' home at 112 Ludlow Street, behind Deering High School. My grandfather would always take in the Deering-Portland football game with some of his cronies. For some reason he never took us kids along and I suspect the flask he always took with him might have had something to do with it. Thanksgiving dinner always awaited his return.

These days, we usually drive to Lexington, Massachusetts, birthplace of the American Revolution and home to my wife Carolyn's sister and her family, for Thanksgiving. On the way, we listen for Arlo Guthrie's Thanksgiving classic "Alice's Restaurant" on the radio and arrive to the smell of a meal already being prepared, pitching in to set the table and help with last-minute preparations.

When all is ready I am often called upon to say the blessing and I usually repeat the same blessing that my Nana Beem used to say at Ludlow Street. "Bless us, O Lord, with these thy gifts which we are about to receive from thy bounty. Through Christ, our Lord. Amen." Then we gorge ourselves on turkey (one year deep fried by my adventurous brother-in-law, a gourmet scientist) and all the fixings, including more pies than anyone should eat at a single meal. Then, under the influence of the turkey's tryptophane, we doze through a televised football game or two before heading north.

Tess and Carolyn sometimes go down to Lexington a day early and come home a day later, but I don't sleep well away from home, so I'm always on the road on Thanksgiving, Thanksgiving Day itself being the best time to travel on the biggest travel holiday of the year.

I think another reason Thanksgiving is Tess's favorite holiday is that it is a holiday gathering without obvious ulterior motives. There is much less anxiety and fewer expectations surrounding Thanksgiving than, say, Christmas, New Year's, and Easter. For while Thanksgiving is nominally a religious holiday, it is not tied to any one religious tradition.

It is simply a day set aside to give thanks for the blessings of life and liberty in these United States.

When I was a child, I somehow thought we were supposed to be thanking the Indians who helped the Pilgrims make it through the first winter in the Plymouth Colony. Then for many years I was just generically thankful on Thanksgiving, my gratitude largely undirected and unexpressed. If anything, I was probably more thankful *to* my family than *for* my family.

As I age, however, I become increasingly aware (just as my grandmother told me I would once I got over being an egocentric teenager) that I owe the blessings of loving parents, the love of a good woman, my delight in my lovely daughters, the comfort of our modest home, the good fortune to have been born and brought up in the relative peace of Maine, the pleasure and privilege of writing for a living, and my overall health and well-being to a higher power. The proper object of our seasonal gratitude is God. But I suppose those who have not yet detected the hand of a Creator at work behind the miracle of creation can just thank their lucky stars.

# WINTER

## THE SNOW IS FALLING!
## THE SNOW IS FALLING!

The older I get, the colder I get. And though I was born in Maine and have lived here for all but five of my fifty-nine years, I am always surprised by the first snows of winter. I tend to think that element of surprise is equal parts innocence and experience. The innocent part of me somehow believes that it's just not going to happen this year. The experienced part of me, the internal clock that just keeps running faster and faster as the years pass, can't quite believe that another winter has rolled around so soon.

As I write this early Saturday morning, the ground is still as bare and hard as iron, but the first snowflakes are already blowing in on an icy wind. These are not the transient squalls of fall, but the slow, ominous warning flakes of things to come. By the time you read this, we will all be bound and buried in a foot or so of drifting snow. If you know what's good for you, you'll make a run for it. Get out while you still can! Save yourself!

Snow hysteria is a relatively new phenomenon here in snow country. It used to be that folks more or less ignored the weather. It's winter in Maine; it's going to snow. Get on with it. But as the state has increasingly filled with folks from away, snowstorms have somehow become dire emergencies. Suburbanites driving four-wheel-drive SUVs that could probably make it to the North Pole and back if there were gas stations on the tundra race to Hannaford and Shaw's to stock up on survival supplies for the long siege ahead. Of course no one has been snowbound in Maine for more than a few hours in modern times, but the panicked pre-storm throngs seem to feel the need for candles, batteries, bottled water, and new snow shovels with each passing storm. Never mind the fact that the supermarkets didn't even close during the ice storm of '98. The snow is falling! The snow is falling!

The media, of course, is mostly to blame for this hysteria, hyping normal weather into natural disasters and whipping up the worst fears of people so out of touch with nature that they fear the end is near if power goes out for a few hours. Today's *Portland Press Herald,* for example, bears the front-page headline "Something Wicked This Way Comes." I know some sub-editor from Seattle is tickled pink with his own cleverness, but it's this kind of hyperbole that prompts people to panic. And I have no doubt that if I turned on the television (You mean it's still working?!), I would find parka-clad Storm Center correspondents reporting in from remote locations to sweater-clad anchors eager for advance word of the coming calamity. School, civic, and sporting events are no doubt being cancelled en masse. Will *The Nutcracker* still go on in the snow? Can the Christmas Fair possibly survive? Triple A flacks and Maine Turnpike Authority shills are warning motorists off the highways. And armies of municipal snowplows are being deployed even as we speak. Uh-oh, it's starting to snow a little harder now!

The only thing that really bothers me about snow is that in recent years it seems to come up the East Coast from the SOUTH! When did that start happening? Aren't snowstorms supposed to come down from Canada or over the western mountains? Does it bother anyone else that they seem to get more snow in Washington, D.C., than we do in Washington County? My limited understanding of this shift in weather patterns is that it has something to do with global warming. I like to think that the disrupted jet stream is dipping down in search of nonbelievers like President Bush and sending the avenging winds and killer flakes into the nation's capital instead of into New England where they belong.

Before the day is over, I will be out there in the driveway with my shovel. Whether I get to use the big, short-handled silver grain scoop or the curved, long-handled snow scraper depends on the amount and kind of snow we get. I love shoveling snow. I really do. There's something very fulfilling about getting outdoor exercise doing a chore that needs to be done, something very satisfying about being able to see your progress, something very soul-refreshing about the sheer normalcy of getting on with life up here in snow country.

## ANATOMY OF A SNOWSTORM

The first signs of an impending snowstorm for those of us who pay little or no attention to the weather are invariably the unexpectedly long lines and missing shopping carts at Hannaford and Shaw's. If there are people in the supermarket you've never seen before, you can bet the Storm Troopers of Channels 6, 8, and 13 have donned their colorful sweaters, cued the ominous music, and whipped up another panic among the aged and those from away.

The snow is coming! The snow is coming! Run for your lives!

There is a flurry of excited activity as snow-fearing suburbanites scurry to lay in a supply of luncheon meat, pinot noir, and DVDs against the long, anticipated siege. Never mind the fact that no one has been snowbound in Greater Portland since about 1952; it's gonna *snow*!

Things quiet down after the supper hour. Darkness falls and with it the first of the promised "precip," maybe a few flurries to start or some freezing rain followed by sleet and snow. The heavy snowfall inevitably falls overnight. Whether the storm howls in on frozen winds or just quietly muffles the night in white, we wake up to the scrape-rumble-and-roar of the snowplow and the electronic flickering of *No School* announcements on televisions that haven't been on in the morning since the kids got out of kindergarten.

Here we are in March and, if there are many more snow days, the kids won't get out of school until July. Maybe it's time to start thinking about trading that perennially useless April vacation for a warm week in June.

Digging out is by now routine, whether by shovel (the only honorable way), snowblower (the obnoxious way), or plow (the choice of the moneyed and powerful). As there is nowhere left to pile the snow, it must be thrown or blown some distance from the drive or walkway. There is a special circle of Hell, however, reserved for people who blow their driveway snow into the street. Municipal snowplow drivers all over Greater Portland keep tabs on these malefactors and report them seasonally to the public works officials in a place where a snowball doesn't have a chance.

By noon, the streets are clear, the sun is out, the kids are bored, and everyone is wishing timid superintendents hadn't been so quick to call off school.

In terms of winter driving, there are two schools of thought about when conditions are worst. The evening of the storm itself, of course, produces dozens of accidents and cars off the road as foolhardy folk in SUVs, pickup trucks, and vans who haven't figured out that four-wheel-drive doesn't help you *stop* a vehicle, race pell-mell along snowy roads, ultimately spinning out this storm or the next. You can drive just about anywhere in any vehicle in any conditions if you go slow enough, but, hey, what's the point of piloting a Suburban if you can't lord it over the meek, right?

The other camp, to which I belong, is far more fearful of driving the day after a storm. Until the roads clear and dry, you have to fight the blinding slush and spray thrown up by convoys of SUVs headed for Hannaford and Shaw's and speeding semis loaded with sock monkeys bound for Wal-Mart. If I had my way, all trucks would be banned from wet roadways at all times. When it comes to emergencies like snowstorms, we have to prioritize. After all, what's a truck-load of sock monkeys compared to my urgent need to get my daughter to soccer practice?

Two days after a storm, the streets are safe and dry and the melting sun has created the perfect conditions for scraping the driveway down to bare pavement in preparation for the next snowfall. We go on like this indefinitely, shoveling the eternal snows, until one day we simply fly away.

Welcome to Maine. Grab a shovel.

## AN AUTO BIOGRAPHY

The first time I saw her, she was standing by the side of the road looking blue and faded. She obviously had a lot of miles on her, but I'm a pretty good judge of quality—I figured a good home and little cosmetic work would do wonders. And I was right. She came from good stock and had a lot of life left in her. I grew to love her solid ways, her dependability, her stoic air of Swedish grace.

We ran around together for a little over a year. I even took her down to Washington during the dog days of August, ten hours on the road in steamy ninety-degree heat, long days in the city, and not one complaint. Maybe I should have realized she was beginning to fall apart that fall when, on a quick trip to New York City, she momentarily lost her grip and almost flipped out on the highway, but I managed to get her under control and we continued on without incident.

Then, just after Christmas, I took her out to Syracuse to visit my in-laws. I should have known she wasn't up to the long journey in such frigid weather, but I was in a holiday mood and just not thinking. She made it to Syracuse all right, but the effort must have taken a lot out of her.

On the coldest morning of the new year, we set out to do a few errands and I noticed right away that she seemed extremely weak. She was coughing and wheezing in the bitter upstate wind, but I figured she'd be okay once she warmed up a bit. I was wrong.

No sooner had we hit 481 than she started to shake all over. When she began to scream and whine, I saw the end was near and tried to make it back to the in-laws'. Then came the death rattle and, with an awful shudder, she seized up and suffered a complete breakdown. Passing motorists slowed, gawked, and pulled around us. There was oil all over the frozen roadway and an icy wind blew away the pall of smoke. It was not a pretty sight.

I tried repeatedly in the days that followed to get help for her, but, in the end, there was nothing to be done. A transplant was out of the question—too expensive and probably ineffective. Specialists in New York and Maine advised me that the six-cylinder engine in the 1976 Volvo was fatally flawed. The four-cylinder engine could easily do 200,000 miles, but the six frequently threw a rod after 100,000. My 265 DL wagon only had 120,000 on her when she died, but then her odometer hadn't worked for months.

The death of the family car doesn't hit you all at once. After the initial shock wears off, there come periods of confusion, anger, and denial. ("But the damn car wasn't even paid for!") Then, as you process your grief, you begin to put your loss into perspective. At times like this, a bit of history can be very helpful, supplying as it does a sense on continuity.

When my parents were married beneath a Windham rose arbor in 1948, the wedding guests arrived in big, black, shiny sedans that looked like they had been designed by an enterprising entomologist. Those substantial Buicks and Oldsmobiles, the *coleoptera* of the automotive genus, were big, heavy, simple machines, as safe and roomy as the post-war years.

The first family car I actually remember (or actually *seem* to remember, for it may be the *telling* rather than the *seeing* I recall) was a pale yellow Plymouth convertible we had in 1951 when my father was stationed in San Diego with the navy. Like all things Californian, that Plymouth was very mellow, laid-back, and not in the least reliable. The only way to get it going was to jump-start it. Though it must have been annoying at the time, there is a note of nostalgic fondness in my mother's voice today when she says, "It's a good thing we lived on a hill."

Most of the cars we owned in my childhood were Fords, colossal Galaxies and sensible Fairlanes, middle-class cars that were somehow more American than the vaguely Frenchified Chevrolets could ever be. Now and then, how-ever, owing to some inexplicable lapse in common sense, we wound up with tiny, tinny foreign jobs—a Morris Minor with a "bonnet" instead of a hood, and a temperamental Renault Dauphine, which was finally donated to Westbrook High School where it was puzzled over and cannibalized by the shop boys.

My grandparents, it seemed, never made automotive mistakes. Bampi Beem, who always looked suspiciously like an Indian to me, bought a new Pontiac Bonneville every two years whether he needed it or not. (Whoever got his trade-ins made out nicely in the used-car crap shoot.) Nana Beem passed away at the age of eighty-six without ever learning to drive. She explained this and many other things about her life by saying that she was a product of the Age of Innocence. Nana Gibson, a woman of proud, independent, almost regal bearing, drove Dodges. Just why it is that the elderly are attracted to Chrysler products is a mystery to me, but it's one of the few unassailable facts of American life.

I figured out the other day that I have owned about twenty cars in the past forty years. The first of these were kid cars, old burn-outs with a little leftover life to kill, which could be picked up for a couple of hundred bucks. The most notorious was a push-button DeSoto that looked like a cordovan saddle shoe. It died somewhere in Scarborough. Another was a little two-seater Nash that died at the curb in front of our house and stayed there, slowly sinking into the mulch of fall leaves, until a civic-minded neighbor arranged to have it towed away.

The first serious car I owned was a 1972 Dodge Dart that had belonged to my parents and which came to me as a wedding present. Belying its sensible pedigree, the eight-cylinder Dart was willfully over-powered for its size and, as a result, provided no traction on slippery winter roads. Precisely because it was a bomb disguised as a proper vehicle, the Dart was in great demand and had a tremendous resale value. As I was commuting to graduate school in Boston at the time and needed a trouble-free car that was good in the snow, I traded the demon Dodge for the first new car I ever owned, a Volkswagen Super Beetle. Uncle Gordie, who was stationed in Germany with the Air Force, imported the first two VW bugs I ever saw, and perhaps it was my youthful fascination with those worldly, exotic vehicles that propelled my purchase. Nothing except a complete lapse in taste, however, explains why I bought that Volkswagen in Pulsating Saturn Yellow with black racing stripes, a competition steering wheel, and Porsche bucket seats. I traded that big, angry bumblebee in as soon as I was out of grad school.

By and large though, my auto biography is a chronicle of conservative, even thoughtful purchases—five Volvos (all used), one Saab (a recollection in miniature of the black beetles of my prenatal 1940s), a baby-blue Pinto wagon, and a spunky little Subaru that rusted out before its time. For some strange reason, daughters Hannah and Nora, then six and five, would not forgive me for trading away the Subaru. Maybe it was because it was *their* first car, though there was something spooky about their fixation on the Subaru's five-star logo and their obsession with brown seatbelts.

But then, hey, what do I know? The only relative on either side of my family who knows the first thing about automobiles is my Uncle Bill, a handyman who ran a service station in his youth. Uncle Bill, let it be said, knows how to care for a car. He once completely disassembled a Corvette engine, took it into his kitchen, and cleaned every last piece with a toothbrush. I, on the other hand, neglect and abuse cars unmercifully. My only explanation for this destructive behavior is that I must be rebelling against the slavery that automobile ownership imposes on those of us who are neither mechanically inclined nor independently wealthy. If only I were clever or courageous enough to do without a car altogether!

As a motorist *malgre lui,* I tend to take a cavalier approach to cars, often buying the first thing that comes along. My strategy for many years was to gamble that they'd last until they were paid for. If I had my druthers (or a great deal of moola), I'd drive a new Volvo wagon, a Jeep Cherokee, or a Prius, like everyone else in Yarmouth, but I balk at paying more for a car than my folks paid for their first house in Westbrook ($14,500, if I'm not mistaken).

At any rate, with my beloved old Volvo still dead in the dooryard out in Syracuse, I broke down and, against my better instincts, purchased a new Volkswagen Jetta, a peppy little stripped-down jobbie that looked more like motorized luggage than a family car. That presented me with two troublesome questions: Does anyone know who, what, or where *Jetta* is? And why did I have the feeling I had just made a $10,000 mistake?

The moral of this story, I guess, is that you should never buy a new car on the rebound. The Jetta wasn't paid off before it, too, died. I have since switched my automotive allegiance from European cars to Asian—a Mazda van, a Subaru Outback, and a pair of Hyundais. Sure the Hyundais are Korean tin cans, but they're cheap and they have the best warranties in the businesses. And ultimately, I guess that's what I want from life—a free ride and fewer worries.

(Lightly revised from an essay that appeared in *Maine Times,* February 5, 1988.)

# HAPPY NANO YEAR

Welcome to 2000-whatever, an otherwise hopeful yet innocuous year that I have decided should be declared the Year of the Nano in recognition of the fact that everything in life seems to be getting faster, smaller, and harder to understand.

Like millions of other Americans, we bought an iPod Nano for Christmas. Now, once we figure out how to download the latest software, synchronize our desktop computer with her iPod, transfer all her CDs to the computer, and purchase individual songs from the iTunes web site for ninety-nine cents each, daughter Tess will be able to carry up to a thousand songs around with her in a device just slightly larger than a credit card. Is that a good thing? I guess it is if it's not lost, stolen, or misplaced.

The compression of information made possible by nanotechnology is truly awesome, yet one of my many reservations about the digitizing and downsizing of American life is that things will get lost. I mean, I was nervous enough back in 1986 when I was forced by the newspaper I was working for to switch directly from a manual typewriter to a word processor.

When I wrote on a typewriter I could understand how the words got hammered onto paper and I could hold my work in my hands. Writing on a computer sure made things easier, but it also meant that I had no idea how or where my work was stored or in what form it existed. I had no sooner gotten somewhat comfortable sending my work in on a floppy disk than I was initiated into the miracle of e-mail, sending my words off through the ether with a blind faith that they would somehow re-materialize when they reached their editorial destination. Now, just last month, I finally purchased a thumb drive in order to back up my files. Also known as a flash drive, this miraculous little gizmo makes it possible for me to store my entire life's work in a techno-container smaller than a Pez dispenser. Imagine how anxious and insignificant that makes me feel.

I tend to resist new technology as long as possible, so it wasn't until last year that we purchased a digital camera, another magical marvel that makes it possible to store five hundred family photos on a matchbook. Frankly, however, I still prefer the twenty-five-years' worth of snapshots and negatives crammed into a couple of large boxes in the base-ment. At least I'm not going to misplace them.

Also this Christmas, I finally broke down and purchased cell phones for Tess and myself. Carolyn and our two older daughters have had them for years, but I had figured that anything I had gotten along without for over fifty years I didn't really need. Whenever Tess would borrow a friend's phone to call for a ride, however, I felt like a mooch, so I fig-ured if I was going to get one for her I might as well have one myself for an additional ten dollars a month. Now I can talk to anyone anywhere in the world on a clamshell, but I'm only giving my cell phone number out to immediate family. My recorded message says, "This is Ed Beem. You've reached my new cell phone. If I can figure out how to answer it, I'll call you back."

I have drawn the line at some new technologies such as instant messaging, text messaging, and PDAs (personal digital assistants such as BlackBerrys and PalmPilots). Admittedly, I am someone who still finds it unfathomable that pictures fly through the air, but I have enough imagination to foresee that one day in the not-too-distant digital future, all of this technology is going to coalesce into an all-in-one media combining Internet, telephone, and television. The logical next step will be the disappearance of the hardware. Then we will all become mobile WiFi beings with little digital diodes planted in our brains.

I suppose I should look at all this nanotechnology as human progress, but, despite succumbing to some of its charms, I remain unconvinced. Carrying a thousand songs in one pocket and your life's work in the other is certainly incredibly ingenious, but I'm still stuck here on the human scale. Just as having the best lawyer in the world is not an advancement over not needing a lawyer at all, so being able to call anyone anywhere at any time on your cell phone is not really an advancement over not needing a phone at all.

Something tells me the greatest luxury in the future will be being completely out of touch. Happy Nano Year!

# LOST AND FOUND

We all have our obsessions, or at least I'd like to think so.
Mine happens to be finding lost or misplaced articles. I wish
I understood why this is, as it would spare my family the
aggravation of the old man turning the house upside down
in search of things of no great value. My mania is such that
family members sometimes conspire to keep from me the
fact that something is missing.

"What are you looking for, hon?"

"Nothing, dear."

"Mom can't find her earring."

(Stage whisper) "I told you not to tell Dad."

Now we are not talking about anything as common as
missing socks, though I will stop whatever I am doing to
match up a pair of socks, no mean feat in a family where little white footie socks seem to multiply and divide in the
laundry.

No, we are talking about things such as jewelry, sports
equipment, clothing, cosmetics, photographs, and books—

portable possessions that can migrate almost anywhere in a house. Not that I limit my searches just to the house. In my single-minded determination to locate the lost I have been known, for example, to search playing fields at night by flashlight, to remove seats from cars, to slip into schools after hours to rummage through lockers and desks, and to comb the yard on my hands and knees. I am no ordinary seeker after lost things.

The thing that's been eating at me for a month or so is that our copy of the history of Thompson Lake went missing at the camp this summer. Having searched high and low, both at home and at the lake, I have more or less concluded that some ne'er-do-well summer guest may have "borrowed" it.

I first discovered my penchant for finding lost items, in fact, back in the 1970s while working at Portland Public Library, where, if I do say so myself, I became quite adept at locating mis-shelved books. Since that time my retrieval skills have mostly been applied to journalistic searches for old files, notebooks, articles, and reviews I have written. This used to be a matter of rummaging through boxes in the basement, but these days it generally involves mousing through endless boxes of backup diskettes.

Lost things offend my sense of order, but I am not a neat freak. I don't mind clutter as long as I know where things are. It seems likely that my lost-and-found mania is some-how related to my obsession with things working properly. If something goes on the fritz—be it a car, a computer, a CD player—I can't relax until I either get the darn thing fixed or get rid of it.

My family tends to regard my fixation with finding

things as some sort of neurosis, but I prefer to think of it as a search for the truth. What I have learned from years of searching is that you will find what you are looking for in the last place you look, but the last place you look may also be the first. It drives me nuts that family members will eliminate a closet, a drawer, even an entire room from the search area after having looked there once. Until you find something, girls, you don't know where it might be, so you can't stop looking in places you've already looked. You may simply have overlooked it.

Perhaps my greatest triumph as a seeker of the lost was years ago when I waded into a muddy farm pond up to my armpits in search of daughter Nora's glasses. (She had jumped out of a rowboat, forgetting she had them on.) The visibility was zero and the bottom a mucky ooze, but I soldiered on manfully through the slime until—Eureka!—I managed to locate and retrieve the glasses with my toes.

I am also quite proud of having once found the cat after everyone else had given up. Nutsy had burned her paws on the engine block of the car (another story altogether) and had slinked off to lick her wounds. We knew she was somewhere in the basement, but no amount of searching or entreaties could locate her. Left alone to search, I was psychically attuning myself to my surroundings when I noticed faint claw marks on the pink foam insulation in a far corner of the cellar. Peeling back some fiberglass batting, I saw the furtive feline secreted in a space between the foundation and the sunroom. Not only had I found the cat, I had found a space that no one even knew existed.

I wish I could give you more specific examples of the things I have spent hours searching for and finding, but one of the things I have definitely lost for good is my memory. I asked Carolyn and Tess to remind me of some of my great finds, but they were, let us say, less than enthusiastic about the task. And now that they have gone off to work and school, I keep having this uneasy feeling that I may have written this column before. Search as I may, however, I can't seem to find it anywhere.

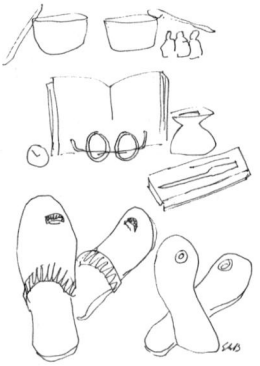

## ALL MY EARTHLY POSSESSIONS

The Great Year-Purge may now drag on into the New Year. The concerted effort to rid the house of the impedimenta of twenty-nine years of marriage and family life (no, not *me*, all the junk we have accumulated) was triggered by the power outage at the end of October during which the sump pump failed and the basement flooded. After hauling off all the soggy carpeting and wet wallboard, I just kept going, so that now I can't seem to stop throwing things away (sorry, *recycling* things).

At first I was just going to clean the cellar. Six carloads of basement clutter—ranging from scrap wood and old bed frames to objects so molded and covered in fuzz from the dryer that I don't know what they might once have been— went to the transfer station in November. Then, being able to see the basement walls and floor for the first time in decades prompted Carolyn to paint them. The new paint job then made all the other stuff in the cellar stand out in bold relief. So inch by inch, foot by foot, I have been working my way through the boxes and bags and odds and ends in an effort to divest myself of everything expendable.

The hardest things to get rid of have been the boxes containing my files. Every magazine or newspaper story I have written over the past twenty-five years has generated a file ranging in thickness from one to six inches. Initially, I was sorting through each box, pulling files and documents I thought I might need again. Then it dawned on me that if I hadn't needed them in twenty years I could probably live without them. So all of my files prior to the year 2000 have now been unceremoniously consigned to the dump.

A more ceremonial purging of the past was reserved for our tax returns and bank records. Carolyn insists on burning confidential documents, so I shoveled a circle in the snow in the middle of the back yard and the three of us—Carolyn, daughter Tess, and myself—had a grand old time consigning all of our financial records from the 1980s to the fire. Stacks of cancelled checks proved the most difficult to burn, requiring constant prodding and separation to get them completely consumed. Ashes to ashes. Easy come, easy go.

You learn a lot about yourself while jettisoning your past. I was amazed, for instance, to see that our entire 1980 tax records fit into a single letter-size envelope. Our 2008 tax info bulges in a padded envelope so large that it barely fits in the file cabinet. There's a lot to be said for living on love.

Today, while hauling a station wagon full of old clothes and bedding to the Goodwill bin, I was reminded of another purging of the past—the weekend in 1987 when the clan gathered to dispose of my Nana Beem's earthly possessions. What started out as a reverential distribution of family treasures ended up in a ruthless discarding of trash, heaving armloads of Nana's junk out the attic window into the dumpster below. I remember thinking that day—as I tossed boxes of cosmetics and costume jewelry out the window—that I was not going to leave behind such a mess for others to clean up once I was gone.

My goal—and I know it will take years to achieve—is to whittle and winnow my possessions down to the bare essentials. My inspiration is a photograph of the earthly possessions of Mohandas Gandhi—a black-and-white still-life depicting Gandhi's two dinner bowls, wooden fork and spoon, two pairs of sandals, glasses, pocket watch, diary, prayer book, letter opener, porcelain statuettes of the Hear No Evil, See No Evil, Speak No Evil monkeys, and a brass spittoon.

I doubt I will ever be able to lighten my material load as much as Gandhi did, though I am buoyed in my attempt by the certain knowledge that the good Mahatma also owned a spinning wheel. I suspect, as well, that he also left a basement or an attic full of archives somewhere on the subcontinent. And personally, I think I could have lived without the porcelain monkeys and the spittoon.

# FIVE COATS OF HISTORY

The hardest thing about surviving a Maine winter is not
staying warm, it's getting dressed. That may sound facetious,
even frivolous, yet as the earth turns and the mercury starts
its hibernal descent, I find the thing I dread most is not the
cold but the nuisance of having to truck with winter clothes
again.

Out of the hall closet come the clutter of mittens and
hats, socks, dickeys, and scarves. Up from the basement the
stumble of boots. From boxes under the eaves come thick,
half-forgotten sweaters smelling of mothballs and last year.
And already the winter coats have begun to escape the closet
in the dining room where they hide out most of the year
with the vacuum cleaner, the sewing machine, and other
unwanted impedimenta of domestic life.

The bother of winter clothes, of course, is one price we
pay for the decision to live in such an inhospitable climate. It
is possible to think of our hairy ancestors plodding through
the snows of yesteryear, barefoot and buck naked, woolly as

bears and wild as wolves, but it was never so. No, Mr. and Mrs. Homo Sapiens surely arose first in gentler climes, extending their range into the hostile territory of snow and midafternoon darkness only as technology allowed.

Why they came at all is beyond me, but rarely do I draw a frozen breath of a bitter-cold Maine winter morning without thinking of the native and natural people of this region. Imagine the fortitude and resourcefulness it took for those Native Americans to survive Maine's brutal winters back when buckskin and campfires were the only sources of heat.

I tend to romanticize the Indian experience, but the first Europeans had it tough, too. Oh sure, some couldn't even hack the winters in Virginia, but it's not as though the European gene pool was all just chicken soup. Think, for example, of that four-thousand-year-old man who turned up in the Tyrolean Alps some years back. Here was a guy older than Moses and tough enough to set out across the mountains wearing nothing but a leather coat and boots stuffed with straw. Were it not for the fact that he wound up frozen solid in the Similaun Glacier, you'd have to applaud his Bronze Age survival skills.

My point here, of course, is that leather doesn't keep you all that warm. If you saw a guy wearing a leather jacket and heading out into a blizzard, you'd feel sorry for him, unless, that is, he happened to be seventeen years old and immortal.

The young simply defy the cold. I've seen it all my life and it continues to be the case. Rebecca, the policeman's artist daughter down the street, used to set off routinely in two feet of snow wearing nothing but China flats. Sixteen years later, our Tess can't be bothered with a coat and often prefers sandals to boots. Getting all bundled up just isn't cool.

When I was in high school in the 1960s, I seem to recall that winter fashions changed annually. One year everyone donned navy pea coats. The next there was a rash of Eisenhower bomber jackets. Then came the fad for army fatigue jackets. The military nature of winter robes past is a bit puzzling, but then this was the 1960s, so I assume we wore our army surplus in some ironic spirit of rebellion.

My pea coat, my bomber jacket (with Thumper the Rabbit stenciled on the left breast by the first love of my young life), and my fatigue jacket all disappeared long ago into the Museum of Lost Youth, along with all my baseball bats, gloves, and trading cards. The only winter coat I retain that even smacks of my youth is the genuine made-in-Austria Lodenfrey stadium coat that dates to my twenties. I only wear it now when the odd mood hits me, and I only keep it because it's a classic. Wearing it, I once fancied it made me look rather European and studious, Young Werther draped in silvery gray wool, an Ivy League Gnossos Pappadopolis (a fictional antihero of my teens). Twenty years older and forty pounds heavier, however, it just makes me look like the family dog wearing a horse blanket.

I am old enough now to remember when the word "parka" was as strange and novel as "Thinsulate" and "Polarfleece." When parkas first came in (c. 1965?), they were mostly worn by women. There was something vaguely feminine about wearing a coat that was so obviously designed to be soft, light, and warm. Now, of course, there's a parka in every pot.

Wandering around the L.L. Bean showrooms, I am dizzied by the array of Baxter State, Cape Breton, North Col, Penobscot, Powderkeg, goose down, warm-up, and warden's parkas, many indistinguishable except for subtle permutations of pockets and insulations. Though my lovely wife works for L.L. Bean, meaning she could get a good buy on any one I wanted, I might be the only person in Yarmouth who does not own an L.L. Bean parka.

For reasons that remain obscure in memory (perhaps having something to do with post-season sales), my parka is a slippery little Christian Dior number, once blue and beautiful, now beaten and faded from a decade of use and abuse. Obviously, this fey jacket was never intended to weather the vicissitudes of a Maine winter, yet other than fading and bagging out (a problem I now share with it), it stood up well to ten years of tobogganing, skating, snow shoveling, and playing in the snow with the kids.

As I contemplate the forced (by Carolyn) retirement of my old blue parka as my primary winter coat, I am faced with the quintessential modern dilemma of whether to go synthetic or natural. Do I want a high-tech, space-age outerwear system? Or do I want a good wool coat? A strong case for the latter is my grandfather's old buffalo plaid Mackinaw that hangs archivally in the closet between the worn-out parka and unworn Loden coat.

My grandfather's Mackinaw has been around a few years longer than I have, dating as best I can tell from around World War II. The cuffs are frayed, the elbows patched, and the lining is but a remnant of its former self, but the main body of the red and black wool is materially intact and worn to a pleasing human texture. My grandfather, from whom I got my name as well as this fine old coat, wore the Mackinaw deer hunting in Washington County and raking leaves in Portland. It has as its chief impersonal qualities the fact that, like all good wool, it stays warm when wet and does not make noise in the woods. Hunters, I am told, still prefer wool, since nylon breaks the stealthy silence with all that swishing.

People who spend a great deal more time in the Maine woods than I do, however, have been won over to synthetics. The Maine Warden Service, for instance, still sports those great hunter-red wool jackets for dress and hunting season, but they winter over in forest-green L.L. Bean Maine Warden's Parkas of DuPont Supplex nylon laminated with Gore-Tex, insulated with Thinsulate, and cuffed with Velcro.

Synthetic materials are also big with the gear guys— skiers, bikers, runners, climbers, campers. Bikers, runners, climbers, and campers seem not to care about appearances (at least judging from the outlandish outfits you see on joggers and cyclists these days), but skiing is obviously as much about looking good as it is about sliding downhill on the snow. The other day, for instance, I saw a fetching little one-piece ski outfit at a ski shop in Freeport. It looked like a cross between a cocktail dress and a wetsuit. I figured anyone who would wear something like that on the slopes couldn't be too serious about the sport, but the ski shop manager set me straight.

"Social skiers—those who drink as much as they ski," he said, "don't wear one-piece suits. It's too hard to go to the potty."

Snowmobilers, however, go to great lengths to stay warm, and they do wear one-piece snowsuits. The alien get-ups they affect make them look like snowbound spacemen and are, for me, proof that man was never meant to snowmobile. No idea how they go to the potty.

I, of course, am a sedentary sort and, despite living in the suburbs, fancy myself something of a city boy. That's why one of my most prized possessions is a luxurious, ink-black cashmere topcoat—just the sort of thing for coming in from the cold while gallery-hopping from one swank opening to another. And the real beauty of this black beauty is that Carolyn picked it up at a church rummage sale for a dollar.

Basically, I go for hand-me-downs and discount chic whenever possible. That's why I love places like Marden's and Reny's. They sell the stuff real Maine people wear in the winter—canvas duck work jackets, insulated hooded sweat-shirts, flannel shirts, long johns, and wool pants so stiff and coarse they'd take the bark off a tree. Fishermen, construc-tion workers, linemen, truck drivers, shipbuilders, Maine hardhats of every description swaddle themselves in layers and layers of cheap, warm, Brand X clothes from discount department stores from Kittery to Fort Kent.

And I suppose that's why I always felt like such an effete dandy whenever I wore the lovely salmon-pink goose down jacket Carolyn bought me some years back. Real Maine men don't wear down, especially pink down. For many years my favorite and most serviceable winter coat was a tan down jacket. All puffed up and tough, it would have done a long-shoreman proud (if there were any longshoremen left in Maine). But then the zipper broke, my waist expanded, and the winter winds seemed to grow colder by the year. I wore the salmony replacement a few times, but I finally asked Carolyn to take it back, complaining that it leaked tiny feathers.

All of which leads me to where I find myself today—

faced with the prospect of buying yet another winter coat. My problem is that I'm neither the ski parka nor the Carhartt and hoodie type. Your clothes say a lot about you, and I'm afraid what my winter coats—Loden, faded parka, grandfather's Mackinaw, rummage-sale topcoat, broken down jacket—say about me is that I'm not willing to spend a lot of money on clothes. Your clothes are an outer expression of your inner being, but right now I'm just being cold.

*Epilogue*: The only changes since this essay first appeared in *Maine Times* in 1991 are that the Loden coat has disappeared and the faded blue Christian Dior parka has been replaced by a black Claiborne Outerwear parka. I assume that's Claiborne as in Liz Claiborne. My only possible defense is that it seems to zip on the proper side. It's also light, soft, and warm. And it was on sale.

(Updated from *Maine Times,* Winterguide 1991.)

## SLEEP IN HEAVENLY PEACE

Sometime Christmas afternoon I will curl up on the sofa in the sunroom and drift off for a pleasant little nap. But then, I drift off into a pleasant little nap almost every day. It is one of the largely unconsidered mysteries of our existence that all living things spend a significant part of their lives unconscious, and the older I get the more I enjoy unconsciousness.

Of course, coming from a long line of nappers, my predilection for a little extra sleep during the daytime is probably genetic. My grandfather and namesake, Ed Beem, used to nap every afternoon in his own sunroom on Ludlow Street in Portland. He'd go in, close the door, cover himself with a wool throw, curl up on the divan with his ornery old cat, and conk out. That's why when I was a kid I thought a catnap meant sleeping with a cat. My father, Al Beem, is famous for being able to catch a little shut-eye wherever he is. On one of the interminable family drives that characterized my 1950s youth, our car broke down and had to be serviced in some out-of-the-way garage. My dad slipped under the car with the mechanic to have a look at the problem. Seeing his legs sticking out from under the car, I remember calling to the mechanic, "Don't let him lie there too long or he'll fall asleep."

Of course, holiday naps such as those routinely taken on Thanksgiving, Christmas, and New Year's are for amateurs. Given a day off, a few drinks, and a little tryptophane from the turkey, anyone can doze off for a while. But try working a nap into every day of your life. That takes creativity, resourcefulness, and a degree of laziness uncommon among productive members of society. And I'm not talking about those New Age power naps popular among the executive class. I'm talking heavy-duty, snore-inflected, dream-laden, drool-inducing midday snooze. I'm talking siesta here, folks.

Siesta, of course, suggests sleeping through the heat of midday, but I'm prepared to nap whenever the opportunity arises. Most of my napping is, in fact, done in the early afternoon, right after finishing the day's writing and right before Tess gets home from school. But I've taken a lot of brunch naps at ten in the morning and plenty of tea-time naps at four in the afternoon. Short winter days, however, present a serious challenge to serious napping. It's hard enough to shake off the cobwebs of afternoon sleep, but if it's light when you zone out and dark when you wake up, you add diurnal disorientation to the usual somnambulant stupor.

Contrary to conventional experience, I do not find naps restorative. Oh sure, nodding off for ten or fifteen minutes can be refreshing, but most of the time I wake up fuzzy-headed and exhausted with a nap hangover. What starts with the warm tingle of surrender (a sensation that has become more pleasurable than a good buzz and almost as pleasurable as sex) invariably ends up leaving me dazed and confused until I get my second wind, usually sometime after supper.

Lately I have taken to setting the kitchen timer for forty-five or sixty minutes, just so I don't inadvertently go on one of those two-hour binge naps that leave you totally incapacitated. Amazingly, despite the profligate nature of my nap habit, I only overslept once during the years when I was supposed to pick Tess up from school. I have, however, had to conduct telephone interviews with some fairly prominent people while not entirely awake. Oddly enough, it didn't seem to make a bit of difference.

Yes, I obviously have some sort of a sleep disorder. I never sleep for more than two hours at a stretch, day or night. I nap out of necessity, not choice. And, yes, I do suffer some guilt knowing that while I'm fast asleep Carolyn is hard at work and the girls are conscientiously going about their work and schooling, but, as I do with all of my failings and weaknesses, I tend to make a virtue of my napping. In an ideal world, we would all sleep whenever we felt like it, not just when we're supposed to. I have simply managed to arrange my unremarkable life so that I have the luxury of selective sleep.

Unconsciousness has a lot to recommend it, and I can't help thinking that we'd all be a lot better off if more people were unconscious more often. So, come Christmas day, try sleeping in heavenly peace.

# FLATTOP WITH FENDERS

As I approach my birthday next week, I have been taking stock of my aging person. Lots of other parts are wearing down and giving out, but I am blessed with a full head of hair. Like most of my other physical attributes however, it is badly neglected.

Being one of those long-haired creepy people from the 1960s, I tend to get my hair cut about once every two to three months whether it needs it or not. I'm not too particular about it, either. I just walk in and tell the woman to "make me look a little more respectable."

Back in the 1950s when I was first old enough to get my hair cut the way I wanted it, I wore one of the many variations of the ubiquitous crew cut. My favorite was a flattop with fenders—buzzed on top, a little wax to keep the front up, and long on the sides so it could be combed back. A flattop with fenders was not to be confused with a flattop with whitewalls, which was buzzed in back and around the ears, making the wearer look rather like a poorly shorn sheep.

By the early 1960s, under the influence of Elvis and Fabian, I was cultivating a pompadour, slicking my hair back constantly into a wave with the omnipresent comb. I must have looked pretty slick, but I could never quite pull off the classic greaser DA. (In polite company, let's just say that DA stood for the part of a duck's anatomy that the back of your hair resembled.)

Though I thought the Beatles looked ridiculous and effete when they first arrived with their Liverpool bowl cuts in 1963, by the time I graduated from high school four years later I was wearing my hair as long as the school dress code would allow. I pushed the collar length and facial hair enough, in fact, to be sent home my senior year to shave and cut my hair. I've pretty much been a shaggy dog ever since.

By the early 1970s, of course, everyone had long hair. If you want a good chuckle, pull out anyone's 1975 yearbook and check out the hair on the boys. It's almost as humorous as the helmet hair on the girls a decade earlier in my 1965 yearbook. If you don't find some Afros and mutton chops, you're probably looking at a yearbook from a military school.

One of the benefits of hanging around for five or six decades is that you begin to see the cycles of life. I'm old enough now that the current vogue for short hair on men looks retro to me. The "high and tight" G.I. cuts in fashion among military and law enforcement officers, the crew cuts and shaved heads of jocks, even the moussed-up short cuts on trendy young execs and messed-up gel cuts on punks and rockers give the twenty-first century a back-to-the-fifties feel.

I've been pleased, however, to see long hair making a

comeback among young men. From caveman Johnny Damon and Samoan gridiron god Troy Polamalu to big-wave surfers and extreme-sport boarders and bikers, some outré males are sporting locks to rival Channel 8 reporter Shannon Moss's trademark Medusan mop.

Short hair on men tends to look unnatural to me, more like a punishment than a preference, but there are limits to my endorsement of long hair. I'm all for 'fros, cornrows, and dreadlocks, for instance, but I am dead set against ponytails. No male born before 1981 should ever, under any circumstances, wear his hair in a ponytail. Ponytails and combovers are just guaranteed to make other people's skin scrawl. Guys, if you're going to creep people out with a middle-aged ponytail, why not just go all the way to gross and get a mullet?

## MORE BLESSED TO GIVE

Like most American men, I am greatly conflicted when it comes time for Christmas shopping. I understand that consumerism powers democracy and I intend to do my part for my country by parting with several thousand dollars, but the older I get the harder I find it is to buy gifts for the people I love.

Daughter Tess is easy enough. Seventeen-year-olds are in the driver's seat when it comes to consumption. Whatever the hot Christmas gift is is what she'll get, and I figure I can't go wrong with anything from American Eagle or on the WCYY playlist.

Hannah and Nora are beyond fashion and fad, however. Just out of college, they are discovering the ugly realities of responsible adulthood—making car payments, paying back college loans, paying for insurance, utility bills, etc. All they really need is money, so that's probably what they'll get, along with a few wrappable gifts such as books, music, movies, or clothes.

Carolyn, though, has always been impossible to please. I suppose I should count the fact that she is not materialistic as one of her many virtues, but no man wants his wife returning her Christmas gift because it is too expensive, the wrong size, wrong color, or just plain wrong. So I plan to do what I do every year—wait until the last possible minute, panic, and buy the wrong thing.

Personally, I'm a big fan of Yankee swaps. You make a game of gift-giving by buying one gift, drawing numbers from a hat to determine an order of selection, and then engage in the politics of give and take—giving the Chia Pet you just opened to someone and taking his or her gift certificate to the Harraseeket Inn, for example. Yankee swaps, however, are fun and funny when done with friends, less so with family—too many emotional land mines if someone actually winds up with the Chia Pet.

Until a couple of years ago, my extended family had been in the habit of drawing names so that we only had to buy a present for one adult. Of course, my mother always subverted the process, because it just wasn't Christmas unless she bought presents for her three sons, even if she hadn't drawn one of our names.

For many years, my immediate family has purchased presents through the church for people in need in the community, but last year my entire family agreed to adopt a family in need instead of buying presents for one another. Carolyn makes the arrangements through a local social service agency and we all go out and buy gifts for perfect strangers, including a food basket for the Christmas meal. All very altruistic of us and very much in the spirit of Christmas, I suppose, but last year I made the mistake of telling Carolyn that I didn't find this charitable act as satisfying as I thought I would. It somehow seemed too removed, too impersonal, too anonymous.

Carolyn immediately jumped down my throat. What the hell was the matter with me? Did I want to deliver the presents myself so I could see the less fortunate people I was helping? She made it perfectly clear that I wasn't supposed to feel good about myself, I was supposed to feel good about helping others. I got the message, babe. It's not that I'm selfish, it's just that I have this nagging suspicion that if I can't pick out presents for people I know and love, I probably made a mess of buying presents for people I only know as "twelve-year-old boy" or "size fourteen mother." I know, I know, it's the thought that counts—more blessed to give than receive, etc.—but I'd hate to think that sweater I bought Size Fourteen Mother was the wrong size, wrong color, or just plain wrong.

Personally, I'm pretty easy to buy for. I don't want for much and I always give the family very specific suggestions when they ask—the title of a book, the kind of socks, the style of underwear. For many years now, I have espoused the steady-state theory of personal possessions—whenever something new comes in, something old has to go. We live in a small house crammed to the eaves with twenty-five-years' worth of the accumulated trash and treasures of a family of five. At this maintenance phase of my life, I prefer to remain material neutral. That's why I like gifts such as food, drink, tickets, and money—things that disappear without taking up permanent space in my little world.

Ultimately, of course, it's not the gift that matters; it's the giving. So I'll do my best to please, but rest assured, I

will not have finished my Christmas shopping when you
read this.

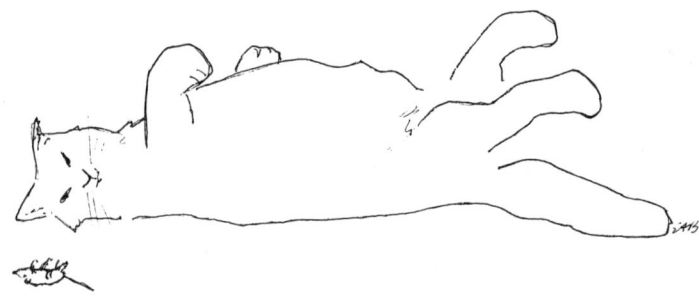

# THE YEAR OF THE CAT

Last night I read a magazine article about a research scientist who believes that cats cause mental illness. Apparently there is some evidence that a virus carried by spores in cat poop may be responsible for schizophrenia. So, all these years, while we thought cat ladies horded herds of cats because they were crazy, in fact, they may have been crazy because they horded herds of cats.

If this theory proves to be true, it would sure explain a lot of things around here. Our cat is definitely making me crazy.

Nutsy is a very needy cat. I should have known that right from the start. Six or seven years ago, when our eighteen-year-old cat Lily went for a long walk and never came back, I went out to the Animal Refuge League to adopt another. I picked out a gray tiger kitten with a very beautiful face, but when I removed her from the cage, her motley, double-pawed sister mewed and cried and muckled onto the side of the cage, pleading with me to take her, too. Being an old softy, I adopted two cats—Nuts and Honey.

Honey was a bold, fearless, independent feline. She spent most of her time outdoors and disappeared into the woods for days at a time. A couple of years ago, she disappeared into the woods for good. I'm pretty sure a coyote must have gotten her, but I have to believe she put up one hell of a fight.

Nuts, on the other hand, is a lazy, fearful housecat. She spends her days looking for the warmest possible place to sleep—a patch of sun, a rug by the baseboard heat, any available lap, or, much to Carolyn's annoyance, the dark recesses of the linen closet. She purrs so loud that you'd swear she was powered by a two-stroke engine, but there is something pathological about that purr. She is constantly hungry, constantly in need of attention, and, once it turns cold, absolutely refuses to go outside.

So the other night, while picking up daughter Nora's room is preparation for her return for the holidays, I hear what sounds like water running. I look over and see Nuts squatting atop a Yarmouth Field Hockey sweatshirt that is soaked in cat pee. Realizing that Nuts must have been using Nora's room as a litter box while she was away, I looked around and, sure enough, found a pile of dried cat poop beside the bed. That's when I went crazy, grabbed the damn cat, and deposited her unceremoniously outside on the back porch.

Cringing and crying, Nutsy slinked off around the corner of the house looking for all the world as though she expected some winged being (an owl? an eagle?) to swoop down and snatch her away. She then spent the entire day sulking in the crawl space beneath my sun-porch office. She did the same thing last winter when I forced her to go outside in the deep snow and, when she didn't come out at the end of the day, we figured she was either too stupid or too traumatized to get out on her own. Carolyn had to crawl out the basement window into the creepy-crawly crawl space to rescue her. This time I think Nutsy realized I didn't care whether she ever came out, so she came out of her own accord at supper-time, as though all were forgiven.

Hey, it's bad enough that our ancient dog Ritz has lost all control of his bodily functions so that I have to tiptoe around the turds when I get up at night and have to wash the kitchen floor first thing every morning, but a cat who willfully soils her master's house—just like a president who willfully violates the public trust—is enough to make you crazy.

# PEACE ON EARTH

Even though I came of age during the Vietnam War, the violence that has defined the history of mankind—and I use the word advisedly, as it is predominantly men who start and wage wars—seemed remote and slightly unreal to me until recent years. Even though high school friends and acquaintances fought and died in Vietnam, I felt removed from the reality of that war in ways I am not and cannot be with the current wars in Iraq and Afghanistan. Somewhere along the line I lost the emotional armor that keeps threats of violence and news of tragedy from sinking in and being taken personally.

Compassion is a sign of a mature and mindful human being, so I guess all I am saying is that I have come late to maturity and compassion. Intellectually I could understand tragedy, but I did not feel it emotionally. When the Ohio National Guard gunned down unarmed student protesters at Kent State University in 1970, for instance, I was outraged at the injustice and took to the streets to protest with thousands of other college students, but I confess I did not feel any empathy for the dead or their families.

In recent years, I find I do not want to hear the particulars of the latest attacks, atrocities, crimes, and disasters, because it has become just too painful, too disturbing. Compassion is uncomfortable. It renders one vulnerable. It used to be that news of someone else's misfortune, suffering, or death prompted a guilty sense of relief that it was not me. Like many if not most young people, I used to think "It can't happen to me." Now I know that not only can it happen to me, it will happen to me—whatever "it" turns out to be.

This awareness of vulnerability and mortality produces both dread and compassion—dread of personal pain and suffering and loss, compassion for the pain and suffering and loss of others. Acutely aware that we are all one human family inhabiting a mysterious and miraculous universe, I now find it totally incredible that human beings can treat one another in the hateful and barbaric ways that are reported daily in the news.

I pray daily for peace—not just the abstract ideal of world peace, but for peace of mind and the peace of Christ that passes all understanding. I would be a servant of such a peace.

It troubles me deeply that religious practices are the basis of so much of the violence and hatred in the world. God knows that there is not one ounce of difference between a Sunni and a Shiite, a Catholic and a Protestant, a Muslim and a Jew, so why don't we, God's people, get along?

Some religious people seem to believe that human tragedy is purposeful, part of a divine scheme. I cannot believe this. I have been taught to believe that God weeps with us at human suffering and that all will be made right in the next world, but I even find that hard to believe. Frankly, I am not a big believer in a next world. I believe in the here and the now and in working to transform this world into the kingdom of God.

That work is not just the work of Christians but of all people of faith. Most of the time, this means putting your faith into action, but on solemn occasions it also means putting your faith into ritual stillness. So on Christmas Eve, just before midnight, I will dim the lights in the church sanctuary as the worshippers raise their candles against the surrounding darkness. Then I will ring the steeple bell to announce the arrival of the Prince of Peace.

Perhaps for that moment there will be peace. Peace be with you.

EDGAR ALLEN BEEM is a freelance writer who lives in Yarmouth, Maine. Former art critic for the *Maine Times*, he has written about art and architecture in Maine for twenty-five years. He is a frequent contributor to *Down East, Yankee,* and *Photo District News,* and he has written for the *Boston Globe Magazine, ArtNews, Design New England, Maine Boats & Harbors, Conde Nast's Traveler,* and *Teacher.* He is the author of *Maine Art Now* and *Maine: The Spirit of America,* and he writes a weekly opinion column entitled "The Universal Notebook" for *The Forecaster,* a Greater Portland weekly newspaper where most of the essays in *Backyard Maine* originally appeared.

For a full catalog of books from Tilbury House, please visit our website at www.tilburyhouse.com